Getting Green

DONE

Getting Green
DONE

Hard Truths from the Front Lines
of the Sustainability Revolution

AUDEN SCHENDLER

PublicAffairs
New York

Hardcover first published in 2009 in the United States by PublicAffairs™,
a member of the Perseus Books Group.
Paperback first published by PublicAffairs in 2010.

PublicAffairs books are available at special discounts for bulk purchases
in the U.S. by corporations, institutions, and other organizations. For more
information, please contact the Special Markets Department at the Perseus
Books Group, 2300 Chestnut Street, Suite 200, Philadelphia, PA 19103,
call (800) 810-4145, ext. 5000, or e-mail special.markets@perseusbooks.com.

Designed by Jeff Williams
Text set in 12-point Adobe Garamond

A CIP record for this book is available from the Library of Congress.
Hardcover ISBN: 978-1-58648-637-2
Paperback ISBN: 978-1-58648-804-8

10 9 8 7 6 5 4 3 2 1

Mixed Sources
Cert no. SW-COC-001271
© 1996 FSC
FSC

The text is printed on ancient forest friendly Rolland Enviro 100 55#
Natural. The paper is made of 100 percent postconsumer recycled content,
was processed chlorine free, and has been certified by the Forest
Stewardship Council, Environmental Choice Ecologo, and manufactured
using biogas. The ink used in printing this book is an environmentally
friendly, vegetable-based ink. The case-making adhesives are water-based,
renewable, and recyclable.

For Ellen, a blessing.

"I'm waiting for that morning
when the new world is revealed."

—"When the Saints Go Marching In"

(New Orleans funeral processions traditionally play
"The Saints" as a dirge on the way to the graveyard.
On the way back, the song becomes a celebration.)

CONTENTS

Shortly after I finished the book in the fall of 2008, there was a political climate revolution in the United States that made even jaded environmental foot soldiers like me optimistic. First, Barack Obama got elected, an eye-watering miracle in itself. Next, he appointed an astonishingly well-qualified dream team to all the most critical climate policy positions. Carol Browner, who understands climate change, its consequences, and policy solutions as well as anyone on the planet, took the new position of White House climate czar. Nobel laureate Stephen Chu, who has been outspoken on the need for drastic action to address greenhouse gas emissions, became head of the Department of Energy. Lisa Jackson took over at the Environmental Protection Agency and immediately made it clear that her agency would regulate CO_2 as a pollutant. Colorado senator Ken Salazar, as clear a thinker on the value of the new energy economy as I've ever heard speak, took over at Interior. And modern-day climate warriors like Cathy Zoi and Nancy Sutley accepted senior positions as well. Meanwhile, what many are now calling "the Great Recession" of 2007–2009 actually reduced CO_2 emissions in the United States, and realities like peak oil suggest that we may necessarily see some level of decline in CO_2 emissions, whether we work to make it happen or not.

This is hugely encouraging news. It even looks like we may enact the most important single policy I call for in this book, the sine qua non of a climate change solution—climate legislation that puts a price on carbon dioxide emissions—within a year.

And yet . . . *after* climate legislation passes, I worry that there's going to be an awful Monday morning when we wake up after a weekend of partying and realize that, yes, policy is in place, and yes, energy costs more—its high price has sent a signal to the markets to get more efficient—and yes, we are on our way. But then what? On that day, as we swill our coffee, we're going to need to reach for the battered glove on the cover of this book. Because in the end, solving climate change is going to be about honest implementation of real solutions and shared stories of all the pain and suffering and glory that entails. Only a brutal openness about how to do this work will enable us to move forward rapidly by learning from each other. That is what this book is about.

One of the greatest challenges we run into in the trenches, as you'll learn here, is that when it comes to confronting the climate crisis, social, cultural, and human barriers to change abound. Even the story behind this book itself is an illustration of the challenges of driving big-scale change.

This book, in part, was an outgrowth of a front-page story about my work in *Businessweek*. The title was "Little Green Lies," and the point of the story was, in theory, that the business community hasn't been entirely forthcoming about the insane difficulty of implementing sustainability. Businesses that are trying really, really hard, like Wal-Mart or Aspen Skiing Company, where I work, aren't succeeding at the only thing that matters: reducing carbon dioxide emissions. Instead, most tout minor green initiatives that make them look good but don't really matter in the long term.

When I got to work the Monday after the article came out, my office was empty: no furniture, no wall hangings, nothing. It was as if I'd been fired. It turned out that clearing my office was a joke on the part of our CFO.

There were other jokes, too. Our vice president of human resources had called me the Friday the article came out and said, "Please see me at the office on Monday morning as soon as you get in." I called his home, called his cell, and e-mailed him, in something of a panic. "If this is about the article," I thought, "I'm screwed. But if it's about something else I'm not even aware of, I'm probably in even bigger trouble. And I really don't want to spend the weekend thinking about this." He finally called me that night, laughing.

It was all pretty funny, but the "jokes" belied a more complex truth. I had screwed up. I had broken a fundamental rule of the corporate world, which a friend explained to me this way: "Businesses want a happy face presented at all times. You didn't do that." While that's true, in Aspen Skiing Company's case it was more that they didn't want to feel attacked by one of their own. I hadn't expressed myself well to the journalist, and so the article misrepresented me. As a result, as progressive as we were, and as supported as I was, few people at Aspen Skiing Company understood what I had been trying to say in the article. After it came out, I had long conversations with many vice presidents about it, and I had to answer pointed questions from the CEO in front of a gathering of some thirty managers. It was painful, and I had a vague feeling of nausea for several weeks afterward. And I lost some credibility in the company.

About a year later, however, I came into my office and discovered on my desk an article torn from *Fast Company* magazine about Patagonia's efforts to reveal the entire ecological footprint of some of its products. On the article, our CEO, Mike Kaplan, who had just returned from a green business conference in California, had scrawled: "Auden, should we be more 'transparent'?"

I hit the ceiling. "Transparency" was exactly what got me into so much trouble in the first place. 1 had tried to speak the truth about the challenges of actually *implementing* green business practices, and look where it got me. Sure, I could have been more eloquent and careful with the press, but in the end the article was a study in transparency. I stormed into Mike's office waving the article.

Mike was laughing. He got it. And at that moment, I had an epiphany:

All along, during and after the publication of the *Businessweek* article, I had assumed that everyone in the company, including the CEO, shared my understanding of sustainability theory, of the desperate need for brutal, even embarrassing, openness. I had mistakenly thought that the sort of self-criticism I was trying for in the article would make sense.

But I had been incredibly naïve. I have spent twenty years thinking about these issues; there's no way I should have expected other managers with extensive backgrounds in other areas, but not necessarily in sustainability, to have my level of understanding, any more than the IT guy should expect me to know how to write code. I was moving too fast: I'd been delinquent in educating employees in the key ideas of sustainable business.

The problem is that my situation is not unique; it's pervasive. Implementing the kind of change that will solve global warming is a slow, grueling process. And it's not even on the radar in most companies. Time is very limited. Yet businesses continue to shy away from transparency. I was recently on a panel with a vice president of environment for GM, and everything that came out of her mouth made GM appear to be God's gift to the environment. It is not. GM has consistently opposed increasing gas taxes, raising fuel efficiency standards, and passing climate legislation. That is changing. But instead of saying "We're great, love us!" why couldn't the VP simply have said: "We are a big, old company—one of the biggest and oldest in the world. We haven't been very progressive over the years, that's true. But we're trying to change, and here's what we're doing." That would have played vastly better than her spiel that created a constellation of eye-rolling in the audience. Why didn't she speak plainly then?

The answer is that, as my friend told me, corporations want everything to be happy smiley faces most of the time, and that's a big cultural obstacle to break down.

In the end, we face a series of major obstacles—barriers to transparency, to new ideas, to new products. And we desperately need to find a way around those barriers so that we can make stuff happen, on big and small scales alike. In effect, we have to overcome a series of "no's."

My old boss Amory Lovins likes to quote Wallace Stevens on this point: "After the final no there comes a yes and on that yes the future of the world hangs." This book is about how you get to that "yes."

ONE

Trench Warfare, Not Surgery

One must imagine Sisyphus happy.

—ALBERT CAMUS

Donnie's Carhartt overalls are so infused with dirt and grease that they crackle when he walks. Lean and haggard and in his fifties, he's got rings under his eyes from fixing balky Snowcats at night in Aspen Skiing Company's vehicle shop. He rarely takes vacations, and he chain-smokes Camels. When I suggested to him once that he might consider using a brake cleaner without a nasty carcinogenic solvent in it, Donnie flicked his cigarette to the ground and said: "*Some*thing's going to get you." Donnie is also a black belt in karate.

Me, I'm an "environmentalist" in a starched shirt. But like Donnie, I've got a job to do. Mine is to reduce the company's impact on the planet and try to make this business "sustainable" to the extent that's possible. Donnie and I ended up in the same shop because the ski resort we work for is trying to operate as a green business. Donnie, and people like him, are the ground troops who are key to solving the world's problems.

I feel an affinity for Donnie's work because I once had a frontline job like his. I used to insulate low-income housing through a government program called Low-Income Energy Assistance. I was a "weatherization technician." It sounds fancy, but it means that I crawled under mobile homes through mud and animal carcasses into spaces so small I couldn't turn my head. Under a trailer, wearing a respirator and a Tyvek suit (basically an air-mail envelope), I learned that everyone becomes a spider expert, and all spiders become black widows.

I poked holes in the floor and blew in boric acid–coated cellulose—a sophisticated name for insulation made from old newspapers. I breathed fiberglass—the next asbestos—while wrapping water heaters. I fell through the ceiling while blowing insulation, landing close to a seventy-year-old man sucking on oxygen.

I did this work in busted towns in western Colorado with names that evoke the hard-as-nails aspect of the work: Rifle, Meeker, Craig, and Silt. "Silt Happens" is the unofficial motto of this last town. "Stop talking and start caulking" was mine. My coworker and I, ourselves living in a double-wide trailer with three other roommates, were on a budget, so we brought lunch every day and ate it in the work van at a highway rest stop. But some days, when things got bleak, we'd splurge on what we called "suicide prevention lunches," buying a burger, fries, and a Coke at a local café. It cut into our box wine budget, but it kept us going.

Every job was dirty, unhealthy, and grueling. And yet, it has become increasingly clear to me that the work I did eighteen years ago was what the front lines of the environmental sustainability movement look like. The work we need to do is neither fun nor sexy, and it sometimes seems impossible. Although I left that job as soon as I could, I stayed in the environmental field, and my trailer insulation experiences left me with an admiration for the trench fighters—the people whose hands are dirty, on the bleeding edge of the problems and the solutions. By necessity, they are the realists. And to be honest, my experience gave me a sense of disappointment in the pure theorists in the environmental movement—the PowerPoint experts who think they know all the answers but haven't ever baked a pie, built a shed, replaced a toilet, or had a newly insulated roof blow off after they installed it, as happened to me. (We forgot to nail it down.)

Realism is important because our problems are more urgent than ever. We don't have time to fool around or to be fooled by the delusion that we're making progress if we're not. We don't have time for theories that aren't grounded in the real world.

The reason for the rush is climate change.

The Climate Crisis Is Happening—It's Here

In November 2007, the Nobel Prize–winning Intergovernmental Panel on Climate Change (IPCC) released its fourth synthesis report, which was signed off on by delegates from 140 countries, including China and the United States. The

New York Times reported that "members of the panel said their review of the data led them to conclude as a group and individually that reductions in greenhouse gases had to start immediately to avert a global climate disaster, which could leave island nations submerged and abandoned, reduce African crop yields by 50 percent, and cause a 5 percent decrease in global gross domestic product."[1] For starters.

The report wasn't news particularly. I had heard as much when I took my first course in climate science twenty years ago. For some time, every single independent scientific body, from the National Academy of Sciences to all G-8 scientific academies, to the American Association for the Advancement of Science, has been in agreement that climate change is happening and is human-caused. It's not as much a consensus as a conclusion drawn by different scientists, using different methods, from different countries, with different ideologies, and speaking different languages, all finding out the same thing. Even the evangelical Christian community agrees and has released the Evangelical Climate Initiative, a call to action signed by many of the most prominent Christian leaders in the United States. And it has become increasingly clear that climate change is about the future prosperity of humankind more than anything else. Climate change is no more an *environmental* issue than it's a global economics issue or a world health issue. Or more accurately, it is just as much an environmental issue.

What *was* new in 2007 was the tone of the report. The IPCC, which was created in 1988 to examine the potential impact of climate change on humans, is known for consensus and understatement—so much so, in fact, that it has often come off as maddeningly mild in its predictions, much to the chagrin of the environmental community. That's why it was unnerving to hear the panel say, in effect, that we need to act now or we risk destroying life on earth as we know it. The organization's leader, a scientist and economist named Rajendra Pachauri (who was appointed by George W. Bush because his predecessor was *too strident on the need for climate action*), said recently: "If there's no action before 2012, that's too late. What we do in the next two to three years will determine our future. This is the defining moment." Nightmarishly, the IPCC's latest dire report didn't include the even more alarming science that came out and the climatic events that occurred in the year it took to complete the synthesis. Recent extensive melting of the polar ice in summer, for example, and the rapid melting in Greenland and West Antarctica had not been predicted by previous models and surprised scientists. Greenland and Antarctica are melting *one hundred years ahead of schedule,* according to Richard Alley of Penn State University.[2] In 2007 the global rise in CO_2 emissions exceeded the most dire predictions of scientists, which means that the models we rely on for a sense of what the future holds are conservative. And yet those "conservative" models suggest catastrophic consequences, some of which look like the big floods and monster storms the United States saw in 2008.[3]

Business: Between a Rock and a Hard Place

Meanwhile, business is both the cause and the victim of environmental decline. Good example: the Chilean sea bass I saw on the menu at a restaurant recently. It will be commercially extinct in two years. Then what do restaurants serve? Better example: At our ski resorts, we will have to make more and more snow to stay in business in a warming climate, which costs us more and more money and uses more and more energy, which in turn warms the climate, requiring us to make more snow. We are cannibalizing the climate we depend on to stay in business, eating our own tail to stay alive. Climate change threatens every business on the planet, and business is the primary cause of it.

As a result, more and more companies, from Patagonia to DuPont, Wal-Mart to GE, are seeking ways to operate without hurting the environment. They are doing this because of the obvious threat, but also because they anticipate a growing desire among consumers for "green" products and services. Equally important, if business is in large part the cause of the planet's problems, then it can also be the solution.

That effort, called the sustainable-business movement, posits that environmentalism and business are a win-win. The consultants—and the literature that's sprung up—say that corporations can have it all: competitive business and clean air, booming sales and biodiversity.

Few have achieved the sustainable-business ideal, but that hasn't stopped the gurus. Their vision: A double green world where environmental stewardship leads to more profits because ultimately the natural world has always been the source of profit. The common refrain is "Green is green." Meaning: "Sustainable business is green both ways—profitable *and* good for the environment!"

The best books in the field—*The Ecology of Commerce, Natural Capitalism, Cradle to Cradle*—have become bibles for green business folk (for good reason). They broadly address solutions and success from the thirty-thousand-foot level. As part of a nascent movement, that is their intent.

The visionaries say we can achieve a new planetary Eden—a place where the concepts of waste and pollution no longer exist, where energy comes from limitless wind and light, and where ecological catastrophes like climate change and fisheries destruction are a thing of the past.

And they are right.

The only problem is that nobody knows how to get there. Or rather, some very smart people have drawn maps, but we don't know the quality of the roads. Or if there even *are* roads. In short, as another reality-based mechanic in Donnie's shop said to me once, "We're strong on the destination, but we're weak on the getting there."

But what happens when we really *try* to get there? When we do some of the things the experts tell us we need to do? Sometimes it's not so pretty. The work is more like trench warfare than surgery.

Donnie's Parts Washer

Back in Aspen Skiing Company's vehicle shop, Donnie agreed to replace his solvent-based parts washer (used to clean bolts and washers, greasy springs, and other mechanical parts) with a water-based model. An aqueous parts washer, as it's called, is a beautiful thing. It's a dishwasher, but for machine parts. Instead of paying for expensive solvents, you use water. Instead of exposing mechanics to toxic fumes, the parts washer uses nothing stronger than citrus-based soap. Instead of paying to have the hazardous waste trucked away, you *eliminate* the waste. And instead of filing complex paperwork to federal regulatory agencies and risking inspection and possible fines, you file nothing because there's nothing to regulate. I calculated we'd get the machine's cost back in eighteen months from savings in solvent purchase and disposal, not even counting the reduced risk and added convenience.

There was just one problem: the washer didn't work. Donnie pulled me aside in his shop.

Looking tired as usual, but in this case also discouraged, he said: "This thing is slow. It leaves a white filmy residue. It sounds like a heavy-metal drummer. What can you do about it?"

After searching for better soap and talking to several repairmen—who told me to try better soap—I was about to give up when an electrician named Dave Draves discovered that the motor was installed backward. Fixed, the machine worked like a dream.

Our project, which was admirable on its merits, almost failed because of something completely unanticipated and unavoidable. It was only our electrician's good will—and honesty—that saved it. (Donnie could have torpedoed the washer, which he didn't really want anyway, by not revealing the problem with the motor.) The misinstallation even risked giving *all* environmental products at Aspen Skiing Company a bad name, further enhancing the widespread feeling that green products may work, but they don't work that well. (Like your environmentally friendly dish soap.)

Here's a dirty secret: sustainable business is hard to pull off. The unforeseen can crush the promise of incredible payback. Personality, custom, politics, and perception conspire to derail change even if the technology to make it happen already exists. The vision is beautiful, but as Bruce Springsteen has said: "Between our dreams and actions lies this world." Difficulties abound. It's just that we never hear about them. Or as engineer Jan L. A. van de Snepscheut has said: "In theory, there is no difference between theory and practice. But, in practice, there is."

On-the-Ground Realities

The great flaw in the sustainable-business movement today is that few are willing to admit that achieving sustainability is difficult, and maybe impossible, without big changes in the way the world currently operates. The gulf between reports, benchmarking, and action is wide and deep; it's called "analysis paralysis." It's always easier to commission another study to figure out just how bad things really are, or what the best ways to solve it might be, than it is to roll up your sleeves and actually start to solve a problem. For many businesses, being "green" means announcing a lot of ambitious programs (none of which have yet happened) and committing to a long process of assessing their carbon footprint. In fact, this is indeed progressive. But that fact in itself is tragic, and it shows just how much the world is stuck on a setting of "business as usual."

One reason for the historic focus on theory and success in the sustainability movement is that to admit failure or missteps in this new field—let alone document them—would present unacceptable cracks in the evolving doctrine. It would be like Linus allowing that the Great Pumpkin might not actually exist.

Government agencies and nonprofits pushing green business have a vested interest in the story that this is a pretty smooth ride: the former are trying to make policy and politicians look good, and the latter are trying to push their mission and raise money based on their success. The same is true for corporations, which are trying either to position their brand or to convince customers and shareholders that what they're doing makes sense and works. Meanwhile, sustainability consultants are reluctant to point out the real-world challenges because they are trying to make a buck on their philosophy. (That's not a criticism—more power to them! And we need more of the effective ones.)

An example comes from the green building world. Stakeholders are often afraid to challenge the myth that environmentally responsible construction is cheap, easy, fun, sensible, and obvious. (It's some, but not all, of the above, yet there are some really good reasons to do it anyway.) The problem is that once you've gone through the green building process, you are scared to point out the warts because your work is now considered a model and you're getting huge PR for it. For example, architect William McDonough, a world-famous green architect, used to give lectures about the Lewis Center at Oberlin College, which he designed. His talks were Pollyannaish even when the building wasn't performing well; he'd make extravagant claims about the energy use (or lack thereof) when the building was in fact using more energy than normal structures. This endemic lack of willingness to admit failure (or even imperfection) prevents the building industry as a whole from learning from its mistakes. And until we overcome that reluctance—until we have conferences about the mistakes we made and the pitfalls we've encountered, not just about the brilliant successes we've had—our learning curve will remain flat.

Dig beneath the surface of one of the many green "success stories" you read about in the news and you'll frequently find something more like *Apocalypse Now* than a finely tuned operation. This doesn't mean we give up. But we need to recognize that it's one thing to watch a PowerPoint presentation on corporate sustainability, and another thing entirely to make it real.

The sustainability gurus say that all obstacles can be overcome. But they generally are talking to people like me who consider it an honor to plunge a low-flush toilet. They haven't had lunch with a restaurant manager whose career depends on his perception of an uncompromised product. I have had that conversation.

There's No Success Like Failure

Imagine for a moment that you are the environmental director at a world-famous resort. After much political wrangling, you manage to install energy-efficient lighting in a high-end hotel restaurant. The project will save thousands of dollars in electricity costs while preventing tons of carbon dioxide emissions from adding to climate change. It's the "rubber on the road" of the sustainability movement, the blue-collar work of the climate battle. The restaurant opens, and the manager is put off by the sight of compact fluorescent bulbs. He removes the bulbs, throws them out, and replaces them with inefficient halogens. Not because he's stupid and ignorant or because he doesn't care, but because he has a business to run and he's doing it the best way he knows how. You don't put energy-efficient fluorescent bulbs in a fancy restaurant any more than you'd put Cool Whip on an éclair.

Nonetheless, this is what your sustainability efforts have brought you: a wasted design and installation fee; inefficient lighting; the manager's loss of faith in green technology; hundreds of expensive compact fluorescent bulbs that, instead of being reused (at the very least), are now leeching mercury out of the local unlined landfill; and unanticipated costs for new bulbs and installation. This is a true story. It happened a decade ago at Aspen Skiing Company. And there's been no improvement in that restaurant's lighting since.

And yet, the existing literature on sustainable business is formulaic: "*Innovative leader overcomes polluting obstacle at a profit—CEO was thinking outside the box!*" Former EPA chief William Reilly touted one recent green business book as "a compelling blueprint for how companies can address critical environmental problems, from climate change to water, and improve their performance, gain competitive advantage, make money, and win friends. . . ." (I'll take two!) In the past decade, *Forbes, USA Today, Fast Company,* the *Washington Post,* cable TV shows, online blogs, and other media have all run articles or shows titled: "It's Easy Being Green!"

It's time for something else. We need a complement to the good books on theory and success. We need something that talks about failure and the difficulties associated with on-the-ground implementation. And the time is ripe. Now that the movement has some momentum, some genuine credibility, and a host of true successes, it's okay to talk about what it looks like in the trenches, even to admit some of the mistakes that have been made along the way. To complement our roadmap to sustainability, we need a book of wrong turns. You don't learn to hit a curveball by hitting it—you learn by missing it.

The good news is that there's nothing shameful about admitting failures. As Oscar Wilde said: "Experience is the name everyone gives to their mistakes." And as McDonough himself said when *Environmental Building News* reported on some problems with the Oberlin structure, with these new projects the point isn't that they work perfectly at first, it's that they eventually work well. "Design is a signal of intention"[4] (including, I would add, the intention to learn as we go). The act of pursuing sustainable solutions is noble; to cover up the mistakes is criminal. We have to be brutally, painfully honest about our work.

An expert, then, isn't a flawless god. An expert is someone who has made all the mistakes in the book and can show you how to avoid them. An expert, by definition, should be profoundly humble.

Aspen Skiing Company's Vision

The restaurant lighting story might lead you to believe that Aspen Skiing Company isn't all that progressive or may not really care very much about the environment and climate. But that's not true.

Aspen Skiing Company's environmental mandate is ingrained in the culture. We have a unique set of guiding principles that steer the company, and one of those principles is "stewardship of our mountain environment." This may sound froofy (so *Aspen!*), but employees can and do slap the principles down on the CEO's desk if we don't follow them. Our core purpose isn't selling lift tickets and hotel rooms, but "renewing the spirit." You can't renew people's spirit if you're destroying the environment, so that gives me, the environmental guy, a seemingly unlimited mandate. (At least that's how I interpret it.)

Many years ago I was at a cocktail party, and one of the owners of the company asked how our toilet retrofit program was going. At the time I wasn't even sure if he knew my name. Most toilets in Snowmass Village had been installed in the 1960s and used five gallons per flush. Swapping them out with 1.6-gallon models could not only save huge amounts of water but also protect Snowmass Creek, the town's water source. And yes, it was true: We had implemented a modest program to do just that.

As fascinating as that may be to the extreme fringe of the environmental community, it's perhaps surprising that ownership would care about it. Our owners either run or sit on the boards of multiple corporations with billions of dollars in market capitalization. They have other things to worry about. But not that night.

Support comes not just from ownership but from senior management and staff. Our CEO, Mike Kaplan, integrates environmental factors into every decision we make on our four ski mountains, two hotels, and golf course. (Recently he banged his fists on the table in front of senior managers and said that he was "extremely anxious" to move aggressively on energy efficiency.) Meanwhile, our company is built around appreciating the natural world. After big snowstorms, I have come to the office only to find an e-mail from Mike saying: "You are a loser if you don't go skiing today." My job—executive director of sustainability—is a senior position in the company. Our CFO, Matt Jones, is my friend; he and I drink bourbon together, and he's almost conspiratorial about protecting the environment, which is good, because he's the one who ultimately finances green projects. Meanwhile, on most days I get calls from some of our 3,800 winter staffers who offer suggestions, attaboys, gentle critiques, and ambitious proposals, from banning smoking in the lift lines to eliminating the toxic perfluorocarbons in ski waxes.[5]

Green Is Tough, Even for the Motivated

Despite our obvious motivation to succeed, every two years we publish a sustainability report that analyzes our energy and emissions. What we've found is that it's really difficult to do what matters most: cut carbon dioxide emissions. Even though we've eliminated millions of pounds of CO_2 through retrofits, green construction, onsite renewable energy, and widespread efficiency measures, our emissions are slowly creeping upward, largely because of growth and the increasing energy-intensity of our business. For example, our fuel use goes up as our guests demand that we improve grooming. Our electricity use increases as we replace old, rickety lifts with more powerful high-speed and high-capacity ones. It's not fair to say that we should just not take these actions—you can't run a world-class resort with forty-year-old chairlifts. At the same time, as we'll see in Chapter 2, scientists tell us that we need to achieve 80 to 90 percent emissions reductions by the end of the century to put the brakes on climate change.

We run into barriers that seem to be universal in the business world. For example, in 2008 our various departments submitted $40 million in requests for capital spending (new roofs, retiling a swimming pool that leaks one hundred gallons per day), but the company only had $9 million budgeted. In this competitive environment, a solar array or an energy-saving heating retrofit might not get funded—and probably shouldn't, given that a roof leaking onto a guest bed needs to be repaired *now.*

Others struggle, too. Wal-Mart, which in recent years has become one of the most progressive corporate leaders on the environment and climate, is spending $500 million annually on green programs. In November 2007, the company released its first sustainability report, which showed CO_2 emissions climbing an average of 8.6 percent from 2005 to 2006.

Writing in the *Atlantic,* Clive Crook noted that, regarding the commitments to cut emissions that countries have made under the Kyoto Protocol:

> With every other rich country signed on [other than the United States] the decades-old upward trend in emissions has not slowed. Japan and Canada are hopelessly above their quotas. In western Europe, only three countries are now on pace to hit theirs. With time running out, others say that they will make the necessary policy changes by 2012, when Kyoto expires—but then, it's easy to say that.[6]

A report from the Institute for Local Self-Reliance on addressing global warming at the local level concluded that, among cities that committed to Kyoto reduction goals, "despite their commitment and their elaboration of significant problems, reducing GHG [greenhouse gas] emissions below

1990 levels will be a major challenge. Many cities will likely fail in their attempts unless complementary state and federal policies are put in place."[7]

Suncor, which used to have the most aggressive stance on climate change in the oil industry, is now involved in one of the planet's great ecological and climate catastrophes—tar sands development in Alberta. What's going on? It appears that business (and government) may well understand the problem but can't do what's necessary—or worse, they don't want to.

Cutting CO_2 emissions is difficult, even for a motivated business or municipality. That's because we live in an energy-based society: We swim in energy like fish in water, and we're equally unaware of it. At the same time, energy has always been cheap, and it still is, even as prices climb, meaning there's limited incentive to conserve it. As a result, businesses cherry-pick the projects that save the most energy at the lowest cost but pass on the deeper emissions cuts necessary to solve the climate problem. In fact, undertaking "cream-skimming" energy measures is what has come to define the implementation of "green business" today.

Business is designed to make money, and making money means creating more carbon emissions, often through growth. Look at Suncor: As soon as the price of oil hit a certain threshold, its climate-saving aspirations went out the window. It went from being the most progressively green oil company on the planet to one of the worst violators in history. Without carbon regulation—a tax on energy or a cap-and-trade program regulating carbon dioxide emissions—

business is always going to default to profit at the expense of the atmosphere, because it costs nothing to pollute. This doesn't mean business is bad. Quite the opposite. Business gives people the prosperity to thrive and provides communities with the tax base to protect the local environment, and anyway, it's not going away. It's one of the oldest human endeavors, perhaps second only to love. What we need to do is find a way to make business a positive force across the board.

Greening corporate America is going to be a slow and difficult process. And it's not clear that we'll have the sort of aggressive government action we need in the short term to correct huge flaws in the free market, like the fact that polluting the sky is free. Case in point: Congress struggled mightily, over a decade, to pass a fuel economy increase of a few miles per gallon. But we know now what we actually need to do on fuel efficiency if we hope to solve the climate problem, and a few MPGs ain't the number we need to hit.

Hitting the "Reset" Button on Society

The scale of the climate problem is so great that to many people it is incomprehensible. Therefore, most plans for action are inadequate. It's fine for people to buy a Prius and use canvas bags at the supermarket, but we can't afford the delusion that such individual action is enough.

My friend Randy Udall, an energy expert who ran a resource efficiency nonprofit for thirteen years, points out that we're not talking about small things here. "*You have to transform the energy system and find another way to fuel prosperity."* Gus Speth, the dean of Yale's School of Forestry and Environmental Studies, echoes this sentiment when he talks about the need to "transform capitalism." We're talking about an enormous undertaking. It means hitting the "reset" button on society. We've done that before—with civil rights, for example, or during the American Revolution. But neither of these massive efforts was under a strict time constraint. One of them—attaining full civil rights—isn't even done. The other involved a war. And solving climate change is at least as tough a challenge as either one.

One way to get at a revolution is through business. I focus heavily throughout this book on the role of business in creating a sustainable world because that has been my primary realm of experience. Corporations have a crucial role to play: Of the one hundred largest economies in the world, fifty-one are corporations. More than individuals, businesses can influence policy because they carry huge weight with government. And businesses can get things done while waiting for policy change to take place.

Still, business is only one key to addressing climate change. Businesses are nimble, motivated (by profit), and powerful enough to drive large-scale change. DuPont, for example, developed an alternative refrigerant that was a huge piece of solving the problem of atmospheric ozone depletion. But even businesses are not going to drive *enough* change, at least not voluntarily. We can't count on them to ride up on a white horse because, at best, most corporations will hit maybe the top thirty percentage points of efficiency, at a relatively good profit, declare success (and it *will* in fact have been a significant success), and then get on with making money. And that's assuming every corporation *cares* about climate change, which not all of them do.

Relying solely on corporate, or individual, voluntary emissions reduction measures to start this revolution is like asking everyone on a becalmed boat to blow toward the sail. It's just not adequate to the task, and not everyone will participate anyway. From where we stand now, with the time constraints and need for massive action, only government action—on a global scale—can drive the level of change at the speed we require.

So why write a book about getting green done on the ground as opposed to just lobbying the government for change? The answer is twofold: First, climate work *simply needs to happen right now. We don't have time to wait.* And second, some of the trench work described in this book does help to create change at very high levels. While we work to make a difference on the policy front (and pushing for change in Washington really does resemble combat), we must begin to act in corporate America and in our own homes, businesses, schools, and communities. Government needs examples of how to be environmentally progressive and case studies from which to build policy. Every individual and business matters because we need labs for determining what's worth pursuing and how best to do it. Although this work is very difficult, the good news is that it only gets easier from here. It only resembles trench warfare now because we don't yet have the policies in place to make it effortless.

Most important, because the time we have to act is so limited, we need to identify what matters and what is fluff and then prioritize. The goal of this book is to help you define *meaningful* action and then get those jobs done. That might mean changing your lightbulbs, but don't stop there. Figure out how you can leverage yourself or your business to drive policy changes at the highest levels—how can you help ensure that everyone on the planet changes their lightbulbs?—and recognize that this work, in the end, will have the greatest impact.

More Grunts, Fewer Visionaries

In sum, we must act now—because we have to, and so that we are ready, with experience on the ground, to move even faster when good policy arrives, good policy that we helped bring about. Through it all, we have to focus on *action,* on actually getting things done. After years of studies and not much change, after small piddling projects that get big press because they're accompanied by huge marketing campaigns, after ineffective or meaningless government programs, and after the thousandth sustainability conference about big ideas that don't contribute anything other than another rubber chicken dinner and a few good cocktails, it's time to buckle down. We need to radically increase the ratio of grunts to visionaries, with fewer grand pronouncements made from podiums and more belly-crawling through the swamps. It's time to crack into the guts of the boiler and tune it up, fix the parts washers, replace the nasty filters in the heating system—and the broken politicians and their broken policies in the governing machine.

This book is about, and for, the implementers—the Donnies—and it is based on the notion that we are all Donnie; we *all* need to be part of an army of foot soldiers, laboring in the trenches, for years, making mistakes, failing, learning, and moving forward, one bloody yard at a time. And then we must go to the bar and *talk* about our experiences, over beers and tequila shots. The stories you'll read here continue the conversation that starts: "How did you do it? What really happened?" This conversation is meant to make our job easier, or at worst to show that none of us is alone in the fight. It's also meant to convert theorists into actors, and that requires the large doses of realism—the straight dope—you'll find in these pages. Understanding what we are in for before we start is essential. If you think you're headed out to play peewee football but the New York Giants are waiting on the field, it would be good to know that up front.

To that end, this book is the story from the front lines you haven't heard yet, because often that story is embarrassing. The goal of the book is to provide a model for understanding and overcoming the challenges of getting green done, to pull the curtain back on the different elements of the sustainability puzzle—from pitching sustainability to supporting clean energy to building green and marketing the heck out of your work—and to show *how* it's done, warts and all. And the book is also meant to help you do the important little stuff while simultaneously working on the bigger issues that, in the end, matter even more.

Aspen is at the heart of many of these stories, providing a sense of one community's role—and fate—so you can figure out what yours might be. Although it may seem strange to focus a book about the dirty reality of sustainability on a place known for glitz and glamour, in some sense that is the point. Solving climate change, as we'll see, is tough work. But it's also beautiful, inspiring, fun, and meaningful. In due time, if it isn't already, the climate field will become glamorous. Especially as we come to realize that the view from the trenches may be the most beautiful of all.

TWO

Climate Change and the Fierce Urgency of Now

> The U.S. should take steps now to reduce emissions in effective and meaningful ways.
>
> —REX TILLERSON. CEO. EXXONMOBIL

Some things never change. You can guarantee that at a high school graduation the valedictorian will quote Dr. Seuss's *Oh, the Places You'll Go!* And at sustainable-business conferences, a speaker, probably the keynote, will try to define "sustainability," always with much hand-wringing about how difficult a task it is. Over the years, whining about what sustainability means has become a cliché. Invariably, speakers use the UN's Bruntland Commission definition: "development that meets the needs of the present without compromising the ability of future generations to meet their own needs."[1] Architect William McDonough says the term should be "sustaining," not "sustainability," the latter term being hard to understand. These definitions work, but the concept is really much simpler.

Sustainability means *staying in business forever*, whatever your business is. If you run a ski resort, that means you have to address climate change while also cultivating your business in many ways. If you're in the business of parenting, to keep that practice viable forever means ensuring clean water, a healthy environment for your children to grow up in, financial security, stable climate, and lots more.

The second you start to think about what it means to stay in business forever, you have to consider a universe of issues. No matter what you do, any level of planetary degradation ultimately threatens your work. Human health as a whole affects both your guests and your employees. Instability and war over natural resources are direct threats to profit. Even global poverty and disease become long-term business issues. It used to be that these were all considered different challenges that needed to be addressed individually. But the advent of climate change as a real, pressing challenge that affects and unites all of the above issues and more has changed the calculus. As Vijay Vaitheeswaran, energy and environment correspondent of the *Economist*, points out in his book *Power to the People*, "with enough clean energy [which is the fundamental solution to climate change], most environmental problems—not just air pollution and global warming but also chemical waste and recycling and water scarcity—can be tackled, and future economic growth can be made much more sustainable."[2]

In short, to stay in business forever, you have to stop climate change.

The Scale of the Climate Crisis

Fortunately, by now most Americans, and most government leaders, understand that climate change is not just a liberal myth but in fact a major threat to civilization. Yet despite the mind-boggling amount of scientific data detailing exactly what's happening, the scope of the problem remains astounding.

If the IPCC report I mentioned in chapter 1 wasn't enough to set your clothes on fire, James Hansen, one of the world's leading climate scientists and the director of NASA's Goddard Institute for Space Studies, has repeatedly said that if we don't take radical action to reduce global greenhouse gas emissions in the next ten years, our children will be living on a planet unrecognizable to us. (He last said that more than two years ago.) He has also said that "we are on the precipice of climate system tipping points beyond which there is no redemption."[3] Weather Channel climatologist Heidi Cullen says, "We know that there are nearly 6.7 billion people on the planet that spill out 2.2 gigatons of carbon; if we continue to spew at that same rate, the climate is going to get a hell of a lot warmer."[4]

Elizabeth Kolbert of the *New Yorker* concludes her book *Field Notes from a Catastrophe* with the chilling comment: "It may seem impossible to imagine that a technologically advanced society could choose, in essence, to destroy itself, but that is what we are now in the process of doing."[5]

Contrary to popular delusion, climate change doesn't just mean that a given area will get a few degrees warmer—creating orange groves in North Dakota, for example. Remember: Only a few degrees Celsius—six or so—were responsible for the ice ages. So a similar amount of warming will influence how crops grow and how human populations will migrate. (If you think Katrina created a refugee problem, imagine a flooded Bangladesh, population 150 million.) Climate change affects the rate of fires and the health of the ocean; access to clean, nonsaline water and to food; and the spread of diseases. In Africa, towns built at altitudes high enough to make them free of mosquitoes are now experiencing malaria outbreaks. Malaria killed one million children last year, mostly in Africa, mostly kids under five.

Because the scale of the crisis before us is so difficult to fathom, the plans for action are inadequate. As Al Gore pointed out in the summer of 2007, not one of the presidential candidates hoping to take over in 2009 had a platform on climate change that was anywhere near adequate to solve the problem. While that changed by the time the parties had their nominees (Barack Obama nailed it, while John McCain drifted off into traditional "drill and burn" ideology), the scale of the problem remains daunting.

One of the best explanations of the level at which we need to work comes from Joe Romm's book *Hell and High Water: Global Warming—the Solution and the Politics—and What We Should Do.* His analysis is based on a famous *Sci-*

ence magazine article by Princeton University professors Stephen Pacala and Robert Socolow. He writes:

> Imagine if the next president, in concert with the U.S. Congress and all the major nations in the world, developed and developing, embarked on an aggressive *five-decade-long* effort to deploy the best existing and emerging energy technology. Imagine that from 2010 through 2060 the world achieves the following astonishing changes:

> 1. We replicate, nationally and globally, California's performance based efficiency programs and codes for homes and commercial buildings. From 1976 to 2005, electricity consumption per capita stayed flat in California, while it grew 60 percent in the rest of the nation.
> 2. We greatly increase the efficiency of industry and power generation—and more than double the use of cogeneration (combined heat and power.) The energy now lost as waste heat from U.S. power generation exceeds the energy used by Japan for all purposes.
> 3. We build 1 million large wind turbines (fifty times the current capacity) or the equivalent in other renewables, such as solar power.
> 4. We capture the carbon dioxide associated with 800 proposed large coal plants (four-fifths of all coal plants in the year 2000) and permanently store that CO_2 underground. This is a flow of CO_2 into the ground equal to the current flow of oil out of the ground.

5. We build 700 large nuclear power plants (double the current capacity) while maintaining the use of all existing nuclear plants.

6. As the number of cars and light trucks on the road more than triples to more than 2 billion, we increase their average fuel economy to 60 miles per gallon (triple the current U.S. average) with no increase in miles traveled per car.

7. We give these 2 billion cars advanced hybrid vehicle technology capable of running on electricity for short distances before they revert to running on biofuels. We take one-twelfth of the world's cropland and use it to grow high-yield energy crops for biofuels. We build another half-million large wind turbines dedicated to providing the electricity for these advanced hybrids.

8. We stop all tropical deforestation, while doubling the rate of new tree planting.

If we succeeded in every single one of these eight monumental efforts, keeping global CO_2 emissions frozen at 2010 levels for 50 years, and then we somehow were able to sharply decrease global emissions starting in 2061, we would stabilize concentrations at about 550 ppm [parts per million]. In this scenario, temperatures would still rise steadily over the course of the century by an additional 1.5 degrees C or more, with further warming after 2100. The Greenland Ice Sheet would likely still melt, with the resulting 20 feet of sea-level rise—but we would have slowed the process significantly and perhaps avoided the worst of the sea-level rise, 40 to 80 feet or more (assuming that we have also adopted strong policies to constrain the emissions of methane and all other greenhouse gases).[6]

Each task Romm describes is an enormous undertaking. Let's briefly take a moment to look at nuclear power and carbon sequestration—two examples of the gigantic challenges we'd face implementing even one or two pieces of the solution.

Given that the United States is the world's second-largest greenhouse gas emitter, we'd be responsible for building most of the seven hundred new nuclear plants under Romm's model. Jon Gertner reported in the *New York Times Magazine* that unless someone starts building new nuclear plants soon, nuclear power in the United States "will begin to disappear in 15 to 20 years, as one plant after another exhausts its operating permit and goes dark. And it will effectively be extinguished as an energy source by around 2050."[7] This is because no new plants have been approved for construction since 1978, and the life of a plant is on the order of fifty years. Just to replace the existing 104 aging U.S. plants would require building a new reactor every four or five months for the next forty years. But it takes many years just to get these plants approved in the first place. Meanwhile, it would take tens of billions of dollars to keep all the existing plants on line (if that's even possible), let alone build any more of them. And we haven't even accounted yet for the fact that nuclear power faces major political and insurability obstacles; has a history of massive cost overruns and shutdowns; has benefited from government subsidies almost equal to the construction costs of the plants; presents a terrorist threat and a seemingly insoluble waste disposal problem; and would not be viable without huge government subsidies that make taxpayers liable for big catastrophes. (Despite all this, nuclear power was a cornerstone of candidate John McCain's proposed climate policy.)

A similar argument can be made for the difficulty of each of Romm's required actions. For example, carbon sequestration (storing carbon dioxide underground) is a key part of the plan, but the technology doesn't exist yet. In his book *The Weather Makers*, Australian scientist Tim Flannery explains that to sequester all the carbon dioxide we produce as a planet, we'd have to inject twelve cubic miles of CO_2 daily* for the next century or two.[8] And even if we pull off everything on Romm's list, we'd merely stabilize atmospheric CO_2, which means we're still getting hotter!

To be fair, some of the solutions seem eminently reasonable. For example, *Scientific American* published an article in the winter of 2007 that showed how the United States could supply 69 percent of its electricity and 35 percent of its total power with solar panels by 2050. To do so would require subsidies of $420 billion by 2050. Given that we're spending $200 billion annually in Iraq—and $700 billion on the federal bailout of Wall Street—that figure seems like a bargain.[9]

....

*Compressed into a liquid, which is how geosequestration works, that volume becomes much smaller but is still awesome in size.

Given the scope of the climate problem and the diversity of the proposed solutions, we must take the time to define which actions are meaningful. Right now, a great deal of energy is being wasted on efforts that make people feel good but miss the point, which is simple and ambitious: *We need to drastically reduce carbon emissions.*

I can't tell you how many calls I get that go something like this:

"Hi, is this the Environmental Department?"

"Yes. How can I help you?"

"Oh, great. I wanted to talk to you about your season passes. Is there a way to recycle those?"

We're talking about pieces of plastic the size of a credit card here. Or sometimes the caller will say: "Can you make them out of corn?"

My response sometimes annoys the caller. "If you are focusing on season passes, you are missing the big picture. In fact, by focusing on the small and irrelevant, you're not just taking your eye off the ball, you're doing active harm to the environmental movement. Because you've become distracted from what matters."

People who get this will pull me aside and say, "Hey, I recycled a can today," just to gig me. It works.

Writer and former MIT linguistics professor Noam Chomsky has talked about why authoritarian-leaning governments love spectator sports—they keep citizens' attention off what really matters. If you're deep into the Broncos statistics, you might not be paying attention to what the government is doing in, say, foreign affairs.

In the Aspen region, a major recent push from one local nonprofit has been to eliminate plastic bags from the grocery store and to initiate a competition with Telluride. Hmmmm . . . the polar ice caps are melting, and the Midwest in the spring of 2008 experienced flooding consistent with twenty years of climate modeling; Denver was experiencing record drought, with only three inches of rain through July 2008; and Grand Junction was about to break a record for consecutive days over ninety degrees. And we're banning plastic bags. To quote John McEnroe: "*You have got to be kidding me!*"

When it comes to environmental issues, the natural human focus on the tangible, the doable—recycling, for example—has become a prime barrier to getting anything substantial done. We can't seem to let go.

But the climate battle doesn't look like a recycled ski pass or a canvas shopping bag. Nor does it look like an off-the-grid house, a car that runs on French fry grease, a Prius, or even a residential solar system. These images aren't irrelevant, but they are only a very small piece of the puzzle—unless and until they happen everywhere, not just in a few wealthy and enlightened enclaves.

Cheney Was Right

Vice President Dick Cheney famously called individual conservation measures like these "a personal virtue" but not the stuff of national energy policy. Installing efficient lightbulbs, he as much as said, may feel good, but it's not going to keep

Montanans or New Yorkers warm. Nor will such action prevent the ice caps from melting. And though it pains me to say this, Cheney was right.

Meaningful action recognizes the scale of the climate problem and responds at scale. We're simply not going to solve climate change by asking *motivated* individuals to drive Priuses, install solar panels, or replace their old refrigerators. There aren't enough of these good people, and the actions they're capable of are ultimately insignificant, even if every single one maxes out their opportunities. Which is not to say we shouldn't take these actions. They are important. It's just that we can't stop there. Unless personal action happens everywhere through policy mandates on a global scale, we're rescuing one teaspoon from the *Titanic*. What matters less is what you personally do to cut emissions; what matters more is ensuring that *everyone on the planet is also doing what you do*. Both actions are meaningful, but the bigger picture is more important and should be our primary focus.

Unfortunately, many of us see personal measures as an endpoint. I recently received an e-mail that was critical of Aspen Skiing Company's environmental work and concluded: "I hope you take my criticism as a passionate reminder that there are a lot of us out there who are leaving the cars in the garage 75% of the time, buying produce from community supported agriculture, reusing EVERYTHING they possibly can, only opening the refrigerator when necessary, keeping the energy efficient radiant heating system at 62 in the winter etc. . . . "

The e-mail concerned me on two levels. One, it smacked of self-righteousness—this person may very well be turning off more people than she's converting. The e-mail writer's tone also conveyed a sense that living one's own life well absolves one of broader action. What's scarier is that the e-mail suggested a complete lack of understanding of the scale of the problem. Despite the desperate need for clarity of purpose in the climate struggle, the vast majority of the American population, it seems, and many in the environmental community, have put their faith in personal action.

This is apparent in the daily discourse: The demonization of the SUV for so many years—an attitude perpetuated by well-intentioned "environmentalists"—is an example of how this tunnel vision is damaging to the greater cause. It's worth exploring this phenomenon so we can understand why a new, broader focus is critical.

SUVs Are Not the Devil

It has long been in vogue to hate both sport utility vehicles (SUVs) and their drivers. The environmental community encourages commando citizens to paste I'M CHANGING THE CLIMATE, ASK ME HOW bumper stickers onto the biggest offenders. A group called Earth on Empty, based in Somerville, Massachusetts, was "ticketing" SUVs for "failure to pay attention to your own behavior," among other crimes, and the Sierra Club, after dubbing the Ford Excursion the *Valdez*, had a hand in the company's decision to mothball the beast. (That and the fact that it got 3.7 miles per gallon in city driving during one test.) A few years ago, Stonyfield Farm Yogurt joined with NPR's *Car Talk* guys on a campaign with bumper stickers that read: LIVE LARGER, DRIVE SMALLER: NOT EVERYONE NEEDS AN SUV. Throughout the nation, the SUV has superseded DDT and big dams on the environmental blacklist. And the religious community has even come up with the WWJD campaign: "What Would Jesus Drive?"

There are good reasons for the anti-SUV bias. Since every gallon of gasoline burned puts twenty pounds of carbon dioxide into the atmosphere, gas-guzzling SUVs are major contributors to global warming. Each five-mile-per-gallon increment in improved fuel economy keeps ten tons of CO_2 from being released over the lifetime of a vehicle.

Global warming aside, sport utility vehicles spew 30 percent more carbon monoxide and hydrocarbons and 75 percent more nitrogen oxides than passenger cars. Those pollutants are precursors to smog and cause asthma and other illnesses. If SUVs got gas mileage equivalent to that of passenger cars, we'd save one million barrels of oil each day. The list goes on.

But despite the strong case against SUVs, the war against them is probably a mistake on the part of the environmental community.

To begin with, most people who drive an SUV, even in a city, probably consider themselves to be outdoors people. It's an identity thing to have four-wheel drive. And outdoors people are often environmentalists. So by vilifying this group, the SUV-haters alienate their own constituents. You may not like driving behind the guy in the Land Cruiser on

I-80, but he's probably voting for open space in his community, supporting wilderness bills, and contributing to the Sierra Club. With a little prodding, he might support even more radical environmental measures. Same with the woman in the Winnebago. But slap a stealth climate change sticker on the bumper, and you've radicalized them. Now they hate "environmentalists" and begin to define themselves as something else.

There's another reason environmentalists shouldn't take the path of "educate thy neighbors about how bad they are." *It's a distraction.* Both industry and government *love* educational "do the right thing" programs. Such efforts put the onus on the public, letting automakers continue with business as usual because they know the forces behind SUV purchases are bigger than any campaign. And government can do what it wants—fight wars, block climate action, torture people—while we berate our friends for tossing an empty Bud can in the trash (or, in Aspen, protest the outdoor fire hearth in the middle of town, which is a bad idea, but ultimately a distraction, too).

This is precisely what Noam Chomsky means when he talks about spectator sports. It keeps the public's attention off what really matters, and their eyes off what the government is doing. During his two terms as president, George Bush absolutely supported a public focus on little things that people could do on a personal, voluntary basis (and he strongly emphasized this approach for businesses as well) because it defused the pressure on him to take any broad policy action.

The anti-SUV campaigns have divided and conquered two groups that both want the same thing: the enviros and the SUVers. People don't drive SUVs because they're bad humans. They do it because there are no other comparably priced vehicles with better gas mileage that offer equivalent perceived safety, convenience, performance, and comfort. People don't want to go home to their kids and say: "I just destroyed a big chunk of the planet today." People generally want to do the right thing, but they make commonsense decisions in the absence of options. Now that they drive an SUV, many of these well-intentioned people feel they can't call themselves "environmentalists" because it would be hypocritical. But it's not their fault—they've been forced into this awkward position by industry and government.

And that is where the environmental community needs to turn its energy to create real change. Environmentalists and SUV drivers may seem as incompatible as wolves and sheep, but even those animal adversaries have common ground: they both want clean air and water, healthy children, a stable climate, and beautiful views.

We just can't afford to alienate an entire group of people on an issue that's not about personal choice, in the end, but about the sort of cars we want to build as a nation. It's not about you, or me, or the soccer mom: it's about all of us working together to demand the kinds of vehicles—and the kind of future—we want for ourselves and our kids.

Yes, we should encourage people to forfeit their SUVs, if we can do it without turning them into Rush Limbaugh listeners. Consumer choices do send a message to business. But since climate policy needs to be enduring, and to be enduring it needs to be bipartisan, we can't risk alienating an entire population that should be on our side.

An Enlightenment-Scale Opportunity

Part of the reason people tend to focus on tangible, individual actions like recycling soda bottles is that the scale of the climate problem is so large that those who do understand it are already half-inclined to give up. What does it mean to cut CO_2 emissions by 90 percent? It's hard to fathom what that world would look like. So a key component of solving the problem becomes attitude. How do we think about climate change in a way that empowers us instead of scaring the pants off us?

First, we can't look at this challenge as the end of the world. Climate change is not the end of the world, but more important, Americans in particular can't be galvanized into action by "the sky is falling" scenarios, even if they're true. We tend not to believe them because we have a compelling history of overcoming predictions of doom with technology or luck (overpopulation, Y2K, and ozone layer destruction, for example). Most problematic, we can't imagine the scope of a challenge like this. The Black Death killed off one-third of Europe, but that was in 1348; we don't have the experience, or social memory, of real catastrophe.

There's another way to look at climate change: As an opportunity on the scale of the Enlightenment or the Renaissance, a rare chance to radically change the face of society forever. Such wholesale societal change is within our ability because we have done it before.

When Europe emerged from the Dark Ages, it moved from a period of irrational superstition—mythology, not reason, ruled people's lives and fear, not optimism, was the operating principle of the day—into an age of reason and rationality. The movement was traumatic, but ultimately it improved every aspect of people's lives, from medicine to law, science to government. Like the Enlightenment, tackling climate change will require a century-long and revolutionary mobilization of society's intellectual resources, finances, mores, vision, government, and technology.

On a highly efficient planet running on clean energy (which is a world that has solved the climate problem), most existing pollution will be gone and many of the obstacles to solving other problems—poverty, starvation, access to clean water (or water at all), disease—will be significantly reduced. Wars will be less likely without the need to fight over scarce resources like oil and water. The health risks associated with contemporary energy generation and usage—mercury in our blood, acid destroying our lakes and forests, diesel fumes in our lungs, toxic smog in our cities—will vanish. And the environment, on which much of our wealth is based, will be able to rebound and flourish when mining, drilling, and clear-cutting are replaced with cleaner, less stressful, renewable options.

When faced with an especially difficult section of river, whitewater kayakers scout the run, examining all the obstacles from the riverbank to plan a safe route through the rocks, holes, and churning waves. At some point, however, most boaters get tired of scouting; anxious to tackle the challenge, they want to get in their boats and go.

We have scouted this climate problem to death. Yes, we are frightened by the immensity of the undertaking. But this is the opportunity of a lifetime, maybe of a species. Like the leaders of the Enlightenment, who viewed themselves as courageous, able, and hopeful, Americans are ready to engage climate change frontally, right now. Because addressing climate change, and the associated work we need to do on energy, is what's for dinner for the rest of our lives, we might as well relish—even enjoy—the battle.

Solving Climate Change Is Like Fighting Ali (in His Prime)

Ooooooookaaaaaaay. But . . . Sweet Jesus! What do we do? The prospect of trying to solve this problem is beyond daunting. It's as if you'd been invited to go into the ring with Muhammad Ali, in his prime, for a fifteen-round bout. The obvious response is: "No thanks." But with climate change, you have no choice—someone has a gun to your head and you've got to fight. So what do you do? One option would be to cower in the ring and let Ali pound you until you die of organ failure. But another approach might be to go for it: Bob and weave, dance and waggle, keep your right up, duck and feint—give it your best shot, maybe even have fun. Pretend you know a thing or two about boxing. Maybe this guy's talk of "hospitalizing a brick" is all bluster. After all, you have no choice. You're still going to get your ass kicked, but at least this will be fun. And at least there's a *prayer* you might get lucky and knock him out.

This is the situation we find ourselves in with climate change. It's not just a story of our time but, to quote ABC newsman Bill Blakemore, "it is the only story."[10] Words that used to have other meanings—like "environmentalism," "government," "parenthood," "citizenship," and "religious faith"—now, just like "sustainability" and "business," mean addressing climate change.

I have a four-year-old daughter named Willa. In public talks, I used to flash her picture on the screen and say that climate change was ultimately her problem. But in the last few years I've realized that it is not her problem at all. She didn't create it, and by the time she's grown up enough to start to solve it, it will be too late. That's in large part because the decisions we make today—building carbon-spewing coal plants with life spans of fifty years or more and inefficient buildings with life spans of one hundred years—not to mention the government policies we create, will affect the indefinite future. This is not Willa's problem. It is ours.

That fact is both daunting and inspirational. It's inspirational in that, just like running the rapids or taking the test, it's sometimes a relief and a comfort to know that the time has come to stop studying and just do it.

Recently, the president of a utility board I've been hounding to do more on renewables agreed that we needed to move but insisted that we should do it slowly. I can't emphasize enough what *New York Times* journalist Tom Friedman says:

"This isn't your parents' energy crisis."[11] Prudence, diligence, and methodically incremental progress has worked for most problems for most of human history (World War II being an arguable exception), but it doesn't fly now. As Eugene Kleiner, a founder of Kleiner, Perkins, Caulfield, and Beyers, has often said: "Sometimes panic is an appropriate response." Let me be clear. It's go time. We can't be timid actors, we must be Vikings running into battle, possibly jacked up on fermented fruit or grain alcohol. We are going to have to break things, and this is going to hurt.

What Matters Most

The writer Paul Hawken has a great response when people ask him if he is optimistic or pessimistic about our ability to confront the climate crisis. He says that if you've looked at the science on what is happening in the world today on the environmental front and you aren't pessimistic, you have the wrong data. But if you meet with some of the people working on these issues all over the world and you're not optimistic, you have no heart.

I used to have a quote by René Dubos on the back of my business cards. It read: "Trend is not destiny." A Renaissance man, Dubos was a French-American microbiologist, experimental pathologist, environmentalist, humanist, and Pulitzer Prize–winning author who is credited with coining the phrase "Think globally, act locally." Dubos devoted most of his life to the study of disease and the analysis of the environmental and social factors that affect the welfare of humans. He helped discover important antibiotics and did groundbreaking research into tuberculosis, pneumonia, and immunology.

He was an optimist, arguing that humans and nature are resilient, increasingly aware of environmental problems, and more able to solve them. "Trend is not destiny" perfectly reflects Dubos's personality and life's work. It is a profoundly hopeful statement.

And yet, it's perhaps too hopeful for the present. Climate change is happening—it's here. Even if we stopped emitting CO_2 completely today, we'd still have a degree or two of warming built into the system. So I've realized that I need a new quote. Something that evokes the need for engagement and courage.

I've ended up with a line from Charles Bukowski, the underground poet, postman, alcoholic, and writer whose gritty, realistic work was wildly popular but never embraced by the mainstream. I have a picture of Bukowski that I also use in slide shows; in it he is smoking and drinking at the same time. He liked to drink, and he liked to fight. And his famous line, which I now have inscribed on my business cards, is this: "What matters most is how well you walk through the fire."[12]

THREE

Sustainability, Fork-Split

And I only am escaped alone to tell thee.

—JOB 1:15–1:19

The Little Nell Hotel in Aspen, Colorado, isn't exactly the kind of place where you'd expect a sustainability revolution to begin. The Nell is America's epicenter of pampering, the country's cradle of luxury. It has ninety rooms with prices that range from $500 to $5,000. Here's the hotel's tagline: "Nestled at the base of Aspen Mountain, the Little Nell blends the virtues of a country inn with the indulgences of a grand hotel." And here's a sense of how rarefied the service is: There are eighty-four master sommeliers in the United States, and nine in Colorado. The Nell has two. It's not uncommon for guests to make what, in other contexts, might seem like outrageous demands of bellhops. Guests regularly pay the staff $30 to keep pets company while they are away. Not to walk them—that would be extra. Not long ago, a private Gulfstream V jet landed in Aspen. The door opened. The stairs were lowered. And a poodle descended. The owner had forgotten her dog. Where was the owner staying? You guessed it. There was the "gentleman" who became outraged and created a huge scene when he did not receive the two pancakes he asked for. (He got three!) There was the woman who gave the concierge $200 (plus a $100 tip) to buy an Easter basket for her daughter at ten o'-clock the night before the holiday because she had forgotten. And then there was the scion of a very famous family who had a fit because his English muffin wasn't fork-split.

You could say the Nell is the poster child for affluence, waste, inefficiency, and decadence. In one sense, then, it's the exact opposite of sustainability. The best hope for a sustainable planet might be to get rid of places like the Nell and other sites of unnecessary affluence. But at the same time, we don't have a magic wand that will make the Nell go away. Nor is it clear where you'd draw the line. Do we dump the Nell but keep Motel 6? Or is Motel 6 a bit much compared to the slums outside of Mexico City and Bangladesh? The fact is that when you spend a dollar in this planetary economy, a portion of that dollar creates more climate-changing carbon emissions. So we're not going to solve this problem by picking and choosing what businesses are acceptable. We have to fix the whole enchilada—so that when you ski, or visit the Nell, or drive to work, your impact on the planet will be radically less than it is today.

Assuming we have to fix all businesses and all economies, no matter how ridiculous they may seem, and recognizing that the atmosphere doesn't care where greenhouse gas pollutants come from, the Nell then becomes something those of us in the field call a "target-rich environment." That's because providing the very best services has traditionally meant throwing a lot of energy at guests. And as a result, saving energy at the Nell is like shooting fish in a barrel. So that's where Aspen Skiing Company decided to start its sustainability work. Despite—or perhaps because of—the fact that you can buy a $10,000 bottle of wine there.

From Think Tank to Parking Garage

When I first came to Aspen Skiing Company, I was fresh out of the nonprofit sector, having received my sustainability education at Rocky Mountain Institute (RMI), one of the leading think—and do—tanks in the sustainability field. If I learned one thing at RMI it was that efficiency is doubly green—good for the bottom line and good for the environment. I also learned that businesspeople are businesspeople. If you offer them a fantastic return on investment (ROI)—30 percent or better—they'll take it. By the time I left, I had taken to heart a line from the institute's founder, Amory Lovins, who called lighting retrofits—which provide better light, energy savings, and environmental benefits—"not just a free lunch, but a lunch you're paid to eat."[1] It was, and is, a justifiable claim, and Amory, by the way, is one of the most important—and accurate—thinkers on the subject of how we solve the climate problem.

On my first day of work I met with the exceedingly well-dressed Nell manager, Eric Calderon. "Here's what we're going to do," I said. "We're going to retrofit all the lights in your ninety rooms with compact fluorescent bulbs." I had

chosen to start with lighting retrofits because they are the
training wheels of the sustainability movement: always very
profitable, usually an improvement, and relatively straightforward. I continued: "They will last ten times as long, so
you'll spend less money on new bulbs, and less staff time replacing them. We'll cut energy use seventy-five percent,
which will get us a payback of less than a year. And best of
all, it's good for the environment, keeping tons of carbon
dioxide [the primary greenhouse gas] out of the air every
year."

Eric said: "No, we're not."

I was baffled. I thought that businesspeople never turned
down good returns. A payback of less than a year was more
than a 100 percent ROI. His response was that he didn't
want guests to come into their expensive five-star rooms and
be greeted with fluorescent lights more reminiscent of an operating room or a janitor's closet. He didn't want that flick-
ering delay, and he didn't want a cold blue light with a
constant hum.

He said: "When you go to Las Vegas and stay in a Motel
6, they have compact fluorescent bulbs. This isn't a Motel 6."

And guess what? Eric was right. He is a stand-up guy
with a viciously good sense of humor. He understands the
need to protect the environment. (Ten years later, Eric is
now a vice president at Auberge Resorts in California, and
he's just commissioned comprehensive energy audits of all
their hotels.) He's my friend. But he's also one of the top luxury hoteliers in the country, and he has a job to do. If he

compromised his product, he'd be out of that job, and then he'd have even less ability to save energy.

In reality, manufacturers had mostly solved the old problems with fluorescent bulbs by the time I proposed the retrofit to Eric, but his aesthetic concerns were real and based on technology from the not-too-distant past. The problem was that while I thought I was proposing a money-*saving* opportunity, for Eric it was also a money-*losing* opportunity, because it threatened the tool he used to generate income—his stylish rooms.

There was another reason Eric didn't want fluorescent bulbs in his hotel.

Every year a secret, mysterious guest arrives at the Nell. That guest is the ExxonMobil five-star (or AAA five-diamond) auditor. He or she dines in the restaurant, samples the wines, chats with the sommelier(s), maybe even asks a bellhop to grab some Chinese food from Little Ollie's down the block. This guest is assessing the quality of the service, the thread count of the sheets, the chocolate on the pillow, and, according to Eric, the quality of the light. "If that auditor sees compact fluorescent bulbs in our rooms, he might downgrade us to four stars." In the five-star hotel world, that's not just a bad thing—that's the apocalypse.

Again, we can't blame Eric for this concern. But most environmentalists do. In turn, they lose a potential ally, and they alienate a good person from their cause. I called ExxonMobil and AAA; they both told me that there's no aspect of their rating system that would downgrade a hotel based on efficient lighting. But that doesn't matter. The chance that an auditor is even subconsciously affected by a perceived lack of quality is too great a risk to take. Paying a few extra bucks on the energy bill is unfortunate. Losing your five-star rating is your career.

My solution was something you'll never hear from the nonprofits or the sustainability consultants trying to make a buck on the great green vision. *I gave up in defeat.*

I told Eric I understood his concerns. And I wouldn't try to retrofit these rooms. Instead, I walked downstairs into the dark, two-level garage.

Scrapping the Easy Bake Oven

There is a children's toy called the Easy Bake oven; those of you over thirty might remember it as the Betty Crocker oven. This device heats small pies and breads using a *light-bulb*. This was always confounding to me as a child. Why did this oven use a bulb, which was designed to give off light, as a source of heat? The goal was to *cook* the food, not light it up. But the reality is this: A lightbulb is a space heater that happens to give off light. And it works through a very roundabout approach: Heat a tungsten filament so much that it actually glows. Using a space heater to provide light is like using a bank of computers to provide heat in your living room—it works, but how clumsy!

The 175-watt lights in the Little Nell's garage were the same sort of beer-keg shape found in high school gymnasiums—the fixtures that take half an hour to warm up (thus the need for

a "gym monitor" to turn them on each morning), hum viciously all day, and turn the gym into a sauna by noon. Unlike high school gymnasium lights, however, the fixtures in
the Nell garage, all 110 of them, *stayed on all the time.*

The lights were responsible for thousands of dollars in
annual expense and hundreds of thousands of pounds of
greenhouse gas emissions. And it turned out that we could
replace those inefficient Easy Bake lights with linear fluorescents for a cost of $20,000. The math looked like this:
After the initial cash outlay, we'd save $10,000 annually in
electricity costs, since the new bulbs and ballasts would cut
the wattage of each fixture by more than half. Equally
good, the new T8 bulbs would last twice as long as the previous lights, and cost one-tenth less to buy. The maintenance staff would spend less time replacing bulbs (and
could attend to guest needs instead, plunging toilets and
arranging for dog care), and less money would be spent on
replacing costly bulbs. Meanwhile, the light quality would
get better.

Once I had all the data collected, I brought my case back
to Eric. I said I'd stay out of the rooms, but why not do the
garage?

His response?

"No."

I was offering a project with 50 percent ROI, a two-year
payback—the kind of deal that I thought businesspeople
simply couldn't refuse. Better, this project had no impact on
guests, since all the cars were valet-parked. In fact, it arguably had a positive impact by freeing up maintenance staff

and providing better light for valets, who had a history of dinging the expensive cars on concrete supports. (The Nell had actually padded the supports with surplus carpeting to avoid the expensive repair bills.) Why in the world would Eric turn this down?

The reason wasn't in any of the sustainability books or inspirational speeches. Eric pointed out that he made money by selling product. His product was a fancy hotel. If he had an extra $20,000 in his budget, he was going to spend that money on high-thread-count sheets, fine leather furniture, additions to the $1 million wine reserves, or improvements to the bathroom fixtures. He was not going to spend those limited capital dollars on something the guests never saw. Here's an example of the same reasoning from another context. At one of our mountains, our property services director, Peter Hoffman, needed to repair a leaky roof. The cost—just to fix the leak, not to do anything fancy and green—would have been $40,000. The mountain manager at the time said, "Shit, I could cut a new trail for that. Fix it for $1,000, and I'll build that trail."

Eric was schooling me in something called "the real world." And yet he is someone who cares as much about environmental issues as I do.

I was battling two issues here: a mental model and the availability of capital. Hotel managers don't believe they make money by saving—they make money by selling. But in reality, a hotel that sells a room only makes a percentage of that sale; the rest is eaten up by overhead—maintenance, utilities, staff, and so on. One hundred percent of energy savings, on the other hand, drop straight to the bottom line and accrue every year, forever. Savings are, in many ways, a much better way for a hotel—or any business—to make money. But it's hard for a five-star hotel to see itself that way. ("Our product is luxury . . . and also energy savings" makes an unlikely magazine ad.)

Selling a new mental model was only part of the problem. I was also battling another very real-world concern: lack of available capital, a problem that always gets short shrift. If the money doesn't exist, all the green philosophy in the world is pointless. This was the situation at the Nell.

Because I understood Eric's position and I couldn't make money materialize, I took the issue to senior management, in the hope that they would find a reserve of cash once they understood the business value of the lighting retrofit.

Demonstrating Energy Savings: John Norton and the Bicycle-Powered Lights

The initial response to the idea from one of the senior managers was: "I don't believe the lights will save money."

"Wait a second," I said. "We're talking physics here. I have engineering estimates on the savings."

"I don't care," was the response. "I still don't believe it."

"But every Fortune 500 company in the world is doing just this kind of efficiency work."

"I don't care. Prove to me that this will save energy." The manager explained that one of his concerns was that we were committing capital based on theoretical returns without any real opportunity for a look back on the actual returns. That capital, in turn, was competing with other projects that either had 100 percent verifiable ROIs or were absolutely necessary, like fixing a leaky roof. This is good logic, not obstructionism.

So I brought two things to the next meeting of the company's senior VPs, CFO, COO, and CEO—a watt-meter and a bicycle.

The watt-meter measured the energy used by a lightbulb with a spinning electricity meter, just like the one at your house. When I put a standard incandescent bulb in the meter, it whirred rapidly around, making a humming sound. I then flicked a switch to power a compact fluorescent bulb. The meter slowed markedly. In fact, it almost stopped moving in comparison.

"I still don't believe we'll see energy savings."

At that point, I asked the COO of the company, an athletic ex-Marine named John Norton, to get onto the bike. The bike was connected to an array of lightbulbs. Using a switch, I could make the bike power four incandescent bulbs or four compact fluorescents. Norton, an avid kayaker, skier, and lifelong environmentalist who now lives in a radically energy-efficient home in Crested Butte, hopped on the bike with gusto. As he labored to power the incandescent bulbs, he began to sweat. I let him go for a while, enjoying myself, and he struggled mightily (though he would deny it) in front of the senior management team. Finally, I pulled the switch and transferred the power he was generating to the compact fluorescent bulbs. His pedaling became effortless. Clearly, the bulbs required less energy.

Then I pulled a trump card: I had pitched the idea of this retrofit to a local nonprofit dedicated to energy efficiency. That organization had a cash fund it used to support projects that reduced greenhouse gas emissions. Our project was so lucrative—if we pulled it off, it would eliminate 300,000 pounds of CO_2 annually, forever—that this organization had agreed to support the project with a grant of $5,000. Now, I told the group, waving a check in the air, if we do this, the ROI goes up to 75 percent!

Someone said: "I still don't believe the savings exist. I want to see the bills go down as a result of the retrofit." This point is certainly legitimate. But it is also true that, more often than not, the very same people who doubt the energy savings potential of lights believe in God. It only illustrates how hard saving energy can be when belief in efficient lighting is sometimes a greater leap of faith than belief in a supernatural being.

The problem here was that all these questions were rational. And I wasn't dealing with eco-destructors either. These were all smart, friendly, concerned, and generally green-minded individuals. But even in a company like ours, it's hard to get past the reality that the only thing that matters in a corporate boardroom is that the bills go down (or the profit goes up). And that's not an evil thing—that's the nature of corporations. They are not established to protect the world.

Unfortunately, demonstrating actual energy savings is much more difficult than you might think. To show definitively that the new lights would save energy, we'd have to spot-meter the garage, putting those lights on a separate circuit. While that's possible, it's also expensive. With electricians billing upward of $100 per hour, installing a spot-metering system would eat into most of our anticipated savings, damaging the strong return-on-investment figures. Meanwhile, if we didn't spot-meter the garage, it was very possible that we wouldn't see the Nell's entire utility bill go down. Why? Because even though the savings from the retrofit were astounding, lighting represented only a small piece of the total electricity bill at the hotel. There were many other loads that had more draw than the lights—electricity ran the refrigeration equipment, snowmelt systems, and ventilation equipment, among other things, including all the other lights in the building. So even a 75 percent savings in the garage might not be reflected in the bills—a colder, darker winter, a change in how food was stored and used, or a host of other events could send the bills higher despite the retrofit.

So what's an environmental director to do? This retrofit had actually been assessed and submitted for five years, and it had been rejected regularly for all the reasons above.

What happened to the sustainability revolution? If we couldn't even do a retrofit with a 75 percent ROI, how could we hope to do some of the more difficult work ahead?

Making Things Happen Sometimes Hurts

Discouraged, I went to the CEO of the company at that time, a man named Pat O'Donnell. Pat was the person who had created our environmental department, and he was the moral force behind the company's greening efforts. He was also a tough guy, having been a lifelong outdoorsman and rock climber, with a specific personal focus on suffering. In his youth, he was on the first American attempt of Annapurna in the Himalayas. It was a disastrous expedition: Half his team died in an avalanche. Pat had hiked the 240-mile John Muir Trail in California alone, without a tent or sleeping bag (one night waking with a bear gnawing on his pack/pillow), because his friends told him that was how you did it. He was sixty-four, gruff, and no-nonsense, shaved his head bald, looked like Jack Welch, worked out for three hours each morning, and came off as a fairly scary fellow to most people. One of his favorite refrains was: "I have a high pain tolerance," which worked its way into conversations in unusual contexts. Once, he told me I didn't have a strong grip. When I protested, I found myself in the middle of lunch in a grip contest with Pat. He crushed my hand, and I crushed back. We called it a draw, but I can tell you now, he won.

"Pat," I said, "what are we doing here? What is the point of the work I'm doing? If we can't pull off this cost-effective, businesslike retrofit, we can't do anything. We should dissolve my department if we're going to be incapable of even the easiest projects."

Pat asked Eric to do the project even if it busted the budget. It wasn't particularly fair, since Eric's budget and planning would be affected, possibly to the detriment of the hotel operations. But to wait a year for the budgeting process seemed like a bad business decision—we'd be leaving a $10,000 bill on the table. So Eric made the retrofit happen.

Shortly after the project's completion, a burglar got into the garage and stole a purse from one of the fancy parked cars. He was running away toward the exit ramp when a maintenance staffer tackled him in a laundry bin. As far as I'm concerned, this was an ancillary benefit of the new lighting. Without the new lights and good visibility, the thief probably would have been able to sneak away. In fact, shortly before the retrofit a valet had driven a Land Rover *through the wall* of the finance department. Poor lighting certainly had something to do with that accident, though management suspected other influences as well.

After the dust had settled, I asked Eric what he thought of the lights. He smiled and said, "They look grand!"

Cascading Benefits of Green

The new lights in the Nell garage were great, but there was another problem: The two-level parking area smelled like sewage.

On the one hand, this might not seem to be a problem— guests didn't go down to the garage, so at worst it was an inconvenience to the staff. But sometimes there was a distinct reek of sewer gas in the Porches, Martins, and Land Rovers the valets drove up to the front door. This would not do, but staff didn't know how to fix the problem. They turned up the garage exhaust fans, to no avail. If anything, the smell got stronger. For the short term, they gave up trying to solve that problem. There were other fish to fry in the engineering department.

One of those fish was bringing the Nell into the modern era of energy management. Not long after the lighting retrofit victory—and partly fueled by its success—a new engineer, with a background in efficiency, arrived at the Nell. He submitted a request for funding to install an energy management system (EMS). In a nutshell, such a system is a computerized brain for the entire hotel. It allows you to see, on a computer screen, exactly what's going on in the hotel at all times. It also allows you to turn equipment on and off remotely, with programmable timers, and to diagnose problems more easily. All new major hotels have this sort of system, but the Nell, having been built on the cusp of this era, didn't have one.

The new engineer showed that such a system had a reasonable payback—about seven years—since the $250,000 installation would save about $40,000 annually in energy costs. The engineer got permission, and a team of contractors installed the system.

Several things became immediately apparent. In the installation process—which involved wiring up everything electronic so that it could "talk" to the central computer—contractors discovered that the snowmelting "heat tape" on the roof (necessary in the winter to prevent dangerous and damaging "ice damming") was on all summer. They turned it off and set the system to turn it off in the spring every year. Sometimes all you need to do to save some energy is gather simple information—or get out of the office.

Next, engineers discovered that the hotel was running three VW Bug–sized boilers at two hundred degrees all the time. That was far hotter than necessary to heat the hotel's water. (Even rich people don't need two-hundred-degree showers.) Not only was this wasteful—something akin to keeping a boiling pot of water on the stove all day in case you want tea—but it was a safety risk: Children, or even adults, risked being scalded in the shower.

Our engineers were able to turn two boilers off and run the remaining one at a more reasonable 160 degrees, instantly saving energy, cutting greenhouse gas emissions, reducing risk, and adding to the hotel's bottom-line profits.

However, there was one problem. Someone at the hotel had recently made a trip to Sun Valley, where there was a hotel with a huge, steaming pool. It was concluded that "we want our pool to steam, too, for ambiance."

"That's easy," said the engineers. "You just turn the heat up to one hundred two degrees Fahrenheit from eighty-five degrees Fahrenheit. Only problem is, you'll have created Aspen's biggest hot tub."

That's what the Nell wanted.

The pool went to 102, and the savings from the boilers went away.

When a staff member suggested that the Nell cover the pool at night, which would save huge amounts of money—the cost of the cover would be paid for in only a few months—the response was: "But then you couldn't see the steam."

This story isn't told to beat up on hoteliers. There are legitimate reasons you might want a steaming pool. One such reason is that the Nell is a business. And it turns out that if you have a warm pool—basically a large hot tub—you sell more high-margin Manhattans from the bar. That's how the pool becomes a profit center, not just a cost. And the income from the whiskey sours is much greater than the cost of the energy use.*

Despite some setbacks, the installers soldiered on. They discovered that the snowmelt on the patios, which ran inefficiently on electricity, was on all the time during storms, at about 130 degrees. For all we knew, it ran like that all winter. There were two problems here: First, to snowmelt a slab, we didn't need to heat it to 130 degrees. Eighty-five would do—all we were trying to do was melt snow, not cook steaks. Second, running it all the time didn't make sense. While slabs take a long time to heat up, they also hold heat for a long time—think of how warm the asphalt is on the highway even after the sun goes down. So we turned down the temperature on the snowmelt and then put the snowmelt on a timer. More energy savings. But here's where the cultural barriers came in.

The Nell's engineering staff (not the chief engineer) didn't like the fact that they had lost control over the snowmelt like that. They wanted to be able to turn it off and on themselves. It wasn't just that they were miffed—if a guest's patio wasn't melting properly, they needed to be able to turn up the heat themselves. What did they do? They hotwired the system so that it was once again running at 130

*General manager John Speers, supported by a new engineer extraordinaire, Mark Fitzgerald, has since turned the heat back down to a reasonable level, gone back to using one boiler, and covered the pool at night. Fitzgerald saved $30,000 in one month just by "turning stuff off and down."

degrees . . . and no longer being controlled by the energy management system.

Joe Nichols, who worked in the Nell engineering department at the time, said: "I've personally been involved with the aftermath of snowmelt not coming on, and it's a nightmare; it's noisy, messy, a big problem. One morning, the snowmelt in the plaza didn't cycle on, and everyone was out front with ice chippers and shovels, hoping we wouldn't get sued." Joe describes chipping snow and ice off one patio, hauling it inside the room into the bathtub, and turning on the hot water to melt it, then cleaning the tub.

A smug environmentalist could say that this is another example of a situation where the technology exists to solve a problem but the culture prevents it from working. But clearly there were good reasons for hot-wiring the system. And there are plenty of other examples of why resistance to the EMS was reasonable. What if there was just a chance . . . the smallest chance . . . that the 160-degree water couldn't deliver warm-enough showers when the hotel reached capacity? That would be a catastrophe . . . was it a risk worth taking? That kind of thought—in the minds of engineers all over the world at this very moment—keeps proponents of efficiency up at night.

One way around this problem—which was ultimately a lack of support at the grassroots—would have been for me, or the chief engineer, to talk to the staff to get buy-in on the project before taking control away from them. This seems elementary, but things are hectic at the Nell—having a sit-down with the staff on projects like this isn't top of mind when people are yelling at you to fix a clogged shower or get some presents up to floor 2 in time for Easter brunch.

Our EMS installation wasn't all bad, however. The installer did analysis that showed substantial energy savings—on the order of $4,000 per month—in natural gas and electricity. Back in the garage, the contractors installing the system noticed that the ventilation fans were running at full speed. "That's odd," they thought. "Garage fans are designed to vent dangerous carbon monoxide fumes. But these fans seem to be venting the garage at a rate appropriate for 1965 Mustangs, not the radically cleaner modern cars mostly parked in the garage." They put carbon monoxide sensors on the fans so that they'd run only when necessary. This not only saved fan energy but kept the heated air in the garage from being vented too rapidly, saving heating energy. It was an elegant solution.

And one more thing happened as a result of this change. The sewage smell went away! It turns out that the fans, running at full speed to vent the smell and the very low levels of carbon monoxide, were pulling sewer gas up from the drains in the floor, causing the stink.

This story about the Nell is decidedly unsexy, but it's an example of the cascading benefits that efficiency sometimes provides, and it's the kind of story that keeps depressive engineers moving forward. Like a Hail Mary bomb or a first kiss, these brief moments of ecstasy and grace, when all things come together magically, are rare and wonderful, and they suggest the presence of a God suitable for engineers. They keep us sustainability guys going.

We need more of these inspiring stories because more often than not our experiences are frustrating. Implementers sometimes find it hard to wake up in the morning; they need to know there's hope.

I came out of the nonprofit sector ready to kick some ass, loaded with tons of ammo from the world of sustainability theory. But at the Nell, during my first project, I came over the top of the trench and got machine-gunned because my ideas weren't grounded in reality—they were fueled by idealism and hope. Those are good traits, but they carry only so much weight in corporate boardrooms.

The leaders of the sustainability movement—the consultants and the nonprofits, even the businesses and the government agencies—almost always paint a rosy picture of the road to sustainability. Beyond the reasons already described, they have to do this partly because it's hard to sell something with a negative campaign. ("This is really hard—actually it sucks—but you should try it!") As my colleague Randy Udall, whose local nonprofit has done its share of implementation, says: "If sustainability were quick and easy, we would have done it already. It's not easy. It's damn hard."

Better to be realistic. "Look, saving energy is difficult and sometimes expensive. But there are some very good reasons to do it, and in the end it will make our business more profitable and durable. Let's move forward."

The consequences of being a Cassandra are severe, because nobody will follow you. But the consequences of being a Pollyanna are no better, because by giving false hope ("Come on, this is easy and profitable!"), you risk losing the confidence of the people who will ultimately drive the change.

A case in point: The clothing company Patagonia once invited in a leading sustainability guru to look at its buildings. The guru, who had awesome knowledge of broad sustainability principles and energy in particular, gave a number of generic suggestions to Patagonia's environmental director. The director then talked with the building engineer, who said: "None of that will work in this specific instance." Thinking he was dealing with standard resistance to change resulting from laziness, ignorance, fear, and human nature, the environmental director asked the building engineer to please explore the feasibility of these ideas anyway.

Four months and $30,000 in consulting fees later, the engineer returned to Patagonia's environmental director with a report showing that none of the ideas were feasible. "We studied this," he said. "None of the ideas are workable here. Thanks a lot, asshole."

Welcome to the revolution, baby.

FOUR

Aspen: A Canary in the Coal Mine and a Shining City on a Hill

> We know what we are, but know not what we may be.
>
> OPHELIA. *HAMLET.* IV.V.43

Where do government and business turn for examples of how to be environmentally progressive? Who's running the beta test? Where is the lab for determining what's worth pursuing? That's where places like Aspen come into play. Despite the fur and leather, the plastic surgery and fancy cars, or maybe because of it, Aspen can be a laboratory, a model for the rest of the world. It's an example of what one community can do to try to find its own biggest lever to drive change. Aspen is a place that can help create a roadmap to sustainability because it has the money and resources to both succeed and fail.

A World's Fair in Progress

At the time everyone believed that the big hit of the 1892 Columbia Exposition in Chicago, the World's Fair, would be the electric dynamo. But it wasn't. The hit of the fair turned out to be the first Ferris wheel, a giant one that met the technological showboating challenge posed by the Eiffel Tower, the hit of the French world's fair.

The fair, Erik Larson writes in *The Devil in the White City*, changed how Americans thought about architecture, what they could expect from cities (the Chicago fair was clean, safe, and beautiful), and what technology could do.[1] To some extent, the fair created modern America—and modern Americans, with their sense that their own ingenuity can change the world, even spin someone to the top of Chicago on a giant, colorful, fragile-looking-but-tough-as-steel pinwheel.

The environmental movement needs something like a world's fair today. We need a series of demonstration projects that will give us experience and inform policy.

We need these examples because environmentalists have been flying white flags on the Internet in the form of despairing essays. One that got a lot of attention, "The Death of Environmentalism" by Michael Shellenberger and Ted Nordhaus, says that the movement's dominant tactic—lawsuits—has failed.[2] The "Death" piece suggests a new approach, but their analysis was roughly a thousand times better than their cure.*

....

*Following their paper, one of the most important lawsuits in the history of the environmental movement, *Massachusetts v. EPA*, which required that the EPA regulate carbon dioxide as a pollutant, was fought and won.

The next paper to zip around the Internet like a bolt of lightning was "Nature's Crisis" by Dave Foreman, a founder of the few-holds-barred group Earth First! He opens with: "In my 35 years as a conservationist, I have never beheld such a bleak and depressing situation as I see today."[3]

His solution? "The bleakness we face is all the more reason to stand tall for our values and to not flinch in the good fight." Foreman suggests that environmentalists, by doing the same things that have already failed, can convince six billion humans to play dead in the interests of wild lands and wild species. A good idea? Perhaps. Likely to happen? Of course not.*

As a result of climate change, we need a new way of thinking, and then living, just as the nation found one a hundred years ago with the help of the 1892 Columbia Exposition. That World's Fair didn't create clean and safe cities, or more exciting architecture, or a sense of what technology could do by itself. But it did bring together what had been spread around in bits and pieces throughout the nation. And it didn't bring those things together to lecture and rant at the audiences. It showed them. It lighted 200,000 incandescent alternating current lightbulbs in a nation where even cities were still dimly lit. And it hoisted people 264 feet into the sky to show them how easily metallurgy and modern engines could transform their view and their way of life.

Those things were revolutionary in 1893, and the visitors to the World's Fair took that vision back to their hometowns.

....

*But you have to love Dave Foreman, a true eco-warrior and a hero of mine.

We live in the towns and cities those turn-of-the-century Americans went on to build.

What we need today is a world's fair that will help us see how we can confront global climate change and associated problems like sprawl, a decimated natural world, and all the other challenges. Happily, such fairs already are under way, and Aspen is one.

When Aspen's Canary Initiative was first launched in 2005, the *Denver Post* reported on this climate change alliance and city program whose founders hoped to make Aspen the leader on research, discussion, and on-the-ground emissions reduction to address climate change; Aspen also hoped to become a sort of mini-Davos, or Kyoto, for the issue over the next several decades.[4] The politely mocking tenor of the article suggested that Aspen's climate emissions reductions were irrelevant—a pygmy of efficiency up against a King Kong of consumption.

This is true. Nobody around Aspen thinks compact fluorescent bulbs are going to hold back global climate change. That's not the point. Taking a lesson from the Danish philosopher Søren Kierkegaard, who thought each existence is the center of the universe (Aspenites are inclined to think that way anyway), Aspen residents have realized that the rarefied nature of their hometown gives them the power to influence the world. Aspen gets press coverage in China, hosts presidents and senators, and, of course, entertains the most influential people on the planet (that is, the people with the most money).

In other words, the Aspens of the world can be seen as a fair that is slowly under construction. Like the Chicago World's Fair, Aspen can be both an inspiration and a lab for innovation. For example, the city of Aspen was one of the first municipalities to levy a carbon tax on buildings larger than five thousand square feet. That policy experience, tested out in the Aspen world energy fair, will inform broader policy. Similarly, our work at the Little Nell can and should influence government policy; we need the government to incentivize sustainability programs to make them easier.

Modern Aspen was started by people who wanted to do more than just let tourists slide downhill on snow. They were tenth-mountain vets: soldiers specially trained in the Colorado mountains who, having fought in Italy during World War II, had just recently, and quite literally, saved the world. Interested in ideas, Chicago industrialist Walter Paepcke founded the Aspen Institute, an intellectual center, in 1950, not long after Bretton Woods changed the global economy. In the 1970s, Aspen pioneered growth restrictions, which created a beautiful town surrounded by open space but also, unfortunately, immensely high housing prices and long commutes for ordinary-income mortals. But that's the nature of an experiment: sometimes it bites you even if it works. The Chicago World's Fair wasn't perfect either.

Today, town council members from all over the country come to Aspen to see the next round in the experiment: a huge number of employee housing units and a very good mass transit system; model child care; an exemplary local foundation that protects community health by looking after its citizens in a multitude of ways; a city that will soon be 80 percent powered by renewables; and an engaged citizenry whose prodigious output of letters to the five local papers drives some residents crazy.

Of course, Aspen has no Ferris wheel or the equivalent of the first lightbulbs. But until now, the city hasn't had the impetus to build any such demonstrations. Now it does. Faced with incomprehensible, and seemingly insurmountable, problems like climate change, it seems we as a people don't quite know what to do. The world has big problems and needs a vision of what is possible that is tied to actual solutions.

With a place to stand, Archimedes believed he could move the world. Aspen is a place to stand. Aspen as a whole is a shining city on a hill: small enough to nimbly change, smart enough to know it's onstage, and beautiful enough to inspire the world.*

Aspen as Metaphor

There's one more reason Aspen is a good model: It is a surrogate for America, a microcosm of all the problems, obstacles, and opportunities we face in the battle against climate change.

....

*The Ferris wheel and World's Fair discussion evolved from conversations with my friend Ed Marston, author, utility board member, small-time real estate maven, and former publisher of *High Country News*. Those conversations turned into an essay we cowrote for the *Philadelphia Inquirer*. Some of the text of that essay is in this chapter, and I thank Ed for letting me use it.

First, Aspen is very much on the front lines of climate change, and the city knows it: That's why it created the Canary Initiative.

One of Aspen's first projects was a study that looked at the best available science to answer the question: What's going to happen to Aspen in fifty years? In one hundred years? The thinking was that a resort community whose economy is utterly dependent on climate ought to have a sense of what the future might hold, if only for basic city planning purposes.

The study's findings were astonishing: Records showed 3 degrees Fahrenheit of warming in the past thirty years, and the best models suggest that the next thirty years hold in store warming of 3.2 to 4.5 degrees under a medium-emissions scenario (meaning much less than the worst-case scenario, based on current trends, for how the world develops and emits greenhouse gas pollutants). This is profound warming. As I mentioned in Chapter 2, the ice ages were caused by about the same fluctuation in global temperatures, but in the opposite direction.

The report also found that even if global greenhouse gas emissions are reduced, Aspen is projected to experience about six degrees Fahrenheit of additional warming by 2100, making its climate similar to that of Los Alamos, New Mexico. If global emissions continue to rise as rapidly as they have been, Aspen would warm fourteen degrees Fahrenheit by the end of this century, meaning that you could click-and-drag Aspen down to Amarillo, Texas.[5]

This kind of change boggles the mind, and it hits the wallet as much as it does the environment. If ski season delay or poor conditions shave 5 to 20 percent off skier numbers by 2030, as the study suggests, then the economic consequences could be significant, with losses ranging from $16 million to $56 million in total personal income (in today's dollars). Though it can't be reliably quantified, poorer ski conditions are likely to affect the resort real estate market in Aspen as well, adding to the losses. Most strikingly, according to the report, "high greenhouse gas emissions scenarios are likely to end skiing in Aspen by 2100, and possibly well before then, while low emission path scenarios preserve skiing at mid- to upper-mountain elevations. In either case, snow conditions will deteriorate in the future."[6]

You could say that Aspen is a climate-based community, a status that extends beyond snow: Aspen's spectacular whitewater rafting in the summer is another major boost to the economy. But if runoffs continue to dwindle and to happen over shorter periods of time, the summer tourist economy starts to collapse. It's already happening. The report showed runoffs occurring earlier, and happening faster, and it predicted more and worse. If you want to know whether climate change is happening in Aspen, ask the people who are intimate with the seasons. Lou Dawson, a legendary backcountry skier who has been touring in the Colorado mountains for thirty years, now says: "April is the new May" in terms of spring snowpack: What you used to find on the backcountry slopes in May, you now find in April. The high peaks have lost a month of winter.

The nearby community of Vail—well known as an alpine destination—is experiencing a warming-induced bark-beetle epidemic in the local lodgepole pine forest. (The bugs survive winters that aren't cold enough, and eventually they kill the trees in which they live.) The trees, historically green, are now brown and soon will be silver. They are all dying. In a short time, Vail may look more like the high desert community of Sun Valley than the alpine forest we have always known it to be. Or it will be repopulated by Aspen trees—a far cry from the spruce and pine forests that gave Vail its alpine feel.

A 2006 Colorado College study called "State of the Rockies" predicted that the legendary ski resort in Taos, New Mexico, would lose 89 percent of its average April 1 snowpack by 2085.[7] As they say in Ms. Pac Man: "Game over." In the summer of 2007, a new annual state-of-the-lake report at Lake Tahoe (which hosts several ski resorts, including Heavenly, owned by Vail Resorts) showed that nights have become warmer, cold days are rarer, and more precipitation is falling as rain instead of snow. The report was based on reliable weather records dating back to 1911, which show that night temperatures have risen more than four degrees Fahrenheit and that the number of days with average air temperatures below freezing has dropped from seventy-nine to forty-two.[8]

But the very fact that changes are already occurring points to a universal obstacle to climate action: willful denial. Many communities like Aspen are reluctant to point out that their economy is, in effect, toast. That fact—never mind the reality of climate change coming true—could hurt the town. People might decide not to buy condos, or they might not teach their kids to ski. (Learning to ski is hard, costly, and time-consuming. Why bother if the snow's going away?)

These are the same concerns that prevented the ski industry as a whole from even mentioning climate change until very recently. When my predecessor, Chris Lane, brought up the issue in a ski industry association meeting in 1999, he was essentially laughed out of the room. Why would a business point out that its future was in jeopardy? It would have been like the typewriter industry announcing around 1980 that it foresaw the arrival of the age of computers.

For business reasons like these, and because of human nature, the inclination to deny that climate change is happening at all is omnipresent in American society in a million forms. (Exhibit A is the oil and gas industry, Exhibit B is the coal industry, and Exhibit C is the federal government, dominated by lobbyists funded by A and B.)

Close to home, take Vail Resorts as an example. A *Time* magazine article in August 2007 cited Aspen's concern about climate change. In the same article, Vail denied that they were seeing any changes. "Less than 100 miles away," the article reads, "Vail officials say they've seen no similar global warming effect." (Even though, as mentioned earlier, the forest in Vail has mostly died around them in the last decade.) "'The Colorado Rockies are in a different situation than the European Alps,' says spokeswoman [Kelly] Ladyga. 'We're situated at much higher elevations—over 12,000 feet at our summits. Seasons have not shortened and our snowfall has been consistent.'"9

While it's true that the relatively high-elevation Colorado ski resorts are likely to fare better than most resorts around the world—certainly better than resorts in Europe and on North America's East and West Coasts—it's also abundantly clear, particularly in the American West, that changes are happening now. The Aspen study was the first in a growing literature on the subject of climate change in the West.

Park City later commissioned a similar study; it found that by 2075 Thanksgiving will no longer be a ski holiday and that midseason snow depths will be 15 to 65 percent lower—meaning an end to Utah's bottomless powder. Throughout the Rockies, atmospheric warming will increase roughly one-third faster than the global mean temperature, which means that most years it won't be possible to begin snowmaking until the end of November.

The studies keep coming.[10] In 2008, the Rocky Mountain Climate Organization (RMCO), in collaboration with the Natural Resources Defense Council (NRDC), released a report that showed:

The American West has heated up even more than the world as a whole. For the last five years (2003 through 2007), the global climate has averaged 1.0 degree Fahrenheit warmer than its 20th century average. RMCO found that during the 2003 through 2007 period, the 11 western states averaged 1.7 degrees Fahrenheit warmer than the region's 20th century average—which represents 70 percent more warming than for the world as a whole. The West has also experienced more frequent and severe heat waves, with the number of extremely hot days increasing by up to four days per decade since 1950.[11]

Vail Resorts' comment, then, isn't a lie per se, but it's a stunningly ignorant statement. The only reason Vail hasn't seen warming is that it hasn't looked. It is hard to see things with your eyes closed, but it's also hard to open your eyes to bad news.

Butcher the Energy Hog

Climatically, Aspen really is a canary in the coal mine. It shows changes and suffers consequences before most of the country, even coastal areas, owing to the unique impact of warming on alpine environments. As such, the city serves a role: the rest of America might learn its fate—or how to avoid it—by watching Aspen in the future.

In the present, Aspen is a good proxy for America as a whole because Aspen is, like the rest of the country, an energy hog. It's the standard-bearer for conspicuous consumption. For that reason, when I mention sustainability and Aspen (particularly skiing) in the same sentence, I often get an "Oh, please!" in response. After all, skiing itself is a completely unnecessary endeavor, and it happens in a place where people have to fly or drive just to get there. Then the visitors typically spend their nonskiing time in energy-intensive houses, hot tubs, hotels, or restaurants—more visions of unsustainability—as they consume avocados, grapes, strawberries—even water—shipped from all over the world.*

The most frequent comment I hear is, "If you care about sustainability, Aspen Skiing Company should just shut down. And the whole town probably ought to shut down, too."

While that argument has some merit, it's ultimately reductionist, and it's also the exact reason why Aspen is such a good surrogate for the country. Certainly Aspen's lifestyle is lavish. But then, so is the entire U.S. lifestyle. You've heard the statistics before: We're 5 percent of the world's population, and we use 25 percent of the planet's resources. Americans burn more fossil fuel per capita than any nation on earth (nearly 1 million btus per person per day, equivalent to 100 pounds of coal, 1,000 cubic feet of natural gas, 8 gallons of gasoline, or one lightning bolt worth of energy per person per day—that's about 26 barrels of oil per person per year).[12]

Meanwhile, a study by the Canary Initiative showed that per capita greenhouse gas emissions in Aspen were about four times the national average. To be fair, that figure was partly the result of including the airport's emissions in the study of the town. Nonetheless, from an energy consumption perspective, if the United States on average is a hog, then Aspen is Hogzilla.

So what do we do? Close down Aspen, then close down the United States? The United States is hugely wasteful compared

....

*Though not so much at the Little Nell anymore, where chef Ryan Hardy established a farm and raises his own animals. He makes cheese, salami, and pâté on-site and grows vegetables locally. Locally raised beef is also sold at the Nell.

to Europe, which, along with the Japanese, uses about 60 percent less energy per capita. And actually, Europe is pretty bad compared to India, which is at the bottom of the energy consumption chart. Do we shut down Paris? In short, there's no way to draw this moral energy line in the sand showing which activities are okay and which are not. In the absence of God-like qualities of judgment over the world, we have to fix the whole system, not pick and choose. Aspen's economy, and China's and Bangladesh's, need to function in ways that are minimally damaging to the earth and to the atmosphere. Down the line, it's likely that businesses like air travel and skiing will go away; they'll just get too expensive. But in the short term, we've got to fix them, not eliminate them.

Furthermore, from a purely practical level, a vibrant economy in Aspen is vital to environmental quality. The Colorado photographer John Fielder published a book of photographs by William H. Jackson from one hundred years ago, complemented with pictures taken in the present from the same location. Looking at towns like Aspen in 1900, you can see that when the economy was based on mining and subsistence, the landscape—and as we know, the watershed and the air as well—was trashed. As Aspen evolved into a vibrant ski economy, things improved. Why? New tax dollars and private money became available for environmental protection and cleanup, open space preservation, nonprofits that protect natural resources, and so on.

This argument has been explored in great depth by Benjamin Friedman in his book *The Moral Consequences of Economic Growth*, which concludes that good times bring out good qualities in Americans—sympathy and generosity—and that environmental success has typically been a result of affluence and surplus.[13] This is a double-edged sword: Vibrant economies have the luxury of protecting the environment, but when things turn sour economically, the environmental program is often the first to get cut.

Yes, modern Aspen emits more carbon, but we also have greater financial resources to address those carbon emissions. It's fair to argue that Aspen *needs* to be a model for the world because, if not us, then who?

We Are All Hypocrites Now

For obvious reasons, many evident in the discussion in this chapter, Aspen is wide open to calls of hypocrisy, something American diplomats hear all the time when discussion turns to climate treaties like Kyoto. In Aspen, what we hear is: "You haven't even started to try to solve your second-home problem, but you announced the Canary Initiative to great fanfare." And globally it's: "You can't ask us to do anything until you Americans deal with your own massive consumption."

In Aspen, local papers are full of accusations of environmental hypocrisy. Here's a sample, posted by alpha6 on aspenpost.net, a local blog:

Every time this topic comes up I point out the hypocrisy of Aspen, only to be attacked for pointing out the obvious. Aspen suffers the same Liberal Limousine syndrome as the rest of the liberals in that the idea is good and as long as someone else sacrifices for the cause. But God forbid that they give up their private jets, their second homes heated to a constant temperature of 72 degrees all year long, their heated driveways, hot tubs, pools, etc., etc., etc. Just look at their "Champion" of this whole Global Warming Crusade, Al Gore, zipping around in a private jet, putting out more emissions in one trip than I would in a whole year, to "get the word out."

Save your hype and sky-is-falling banter for your idiot liberal friends who you are hoping will make changes so they [*sic*] don't have to. Yeah, the world may be warming up, but don't expect the liberals to be the ones to save it, they appear to be to [*sic*] busy accelerating the process to really give a damn. (I mean, you can't expect Nancy Polosi [*sic*] to not want a bigger jet, I mean, how in the world can she go from place to place without her fan club?) Hypocrites? You betcha!![14]

It is criminally easy to accuse people of hypocrisy. But the accusation almost always misses the point, because by virtue of living in a carbon-based economy, none of us can say anything about emissions reduction without being hypocrites ourselves. Existing in the modern world creates carbon emissions. It's just a question of how bad a hypocrite you are. Attacking Al Gore for the size of his house, for example, is merely a Rovian tactic: Suddenly the conversation goes from the global climate crisis—a dire issue threatening all of humanity—to Al Gore's house, which is perhaps of some significance but exponentially less so.

Ironically, in the corporate world it's possible that flagrant hypocrisy, like that exhibited in Aspen and America, is actually *good* for the environment, because it drives change, no matter how uncomfortably. I address this idea in detail in Chapter 9.

To lessen the charges of hypocrisy that could be brought against any of us, it seems obvious that the best thing to do would be to implement even more sustainable practices— the real ones, things that really matter and drive real change. To do that you need to be clear-eyed about how you can make a real difference: you need to find your biggest lever and use it.

FIVE

Finding Your Biggest Lever

Give me a lever long enough and
a fulcrum on which to place it,
and I shall move the world.

—ARCHIMEDES

I get a nightmarishly recurring call from businesses trying to go green, and it goes something like this: "I work with a [hotel management group, property management firm, Fortune 500 business . . . fill in the blank]." The caller wants to sit down and talk about how they could be "greener." "What do you mean by that?" I ask. "You know," the caller says, "recycled paper and stuff like that." Then I usually say something like, "If that level of 'greening' is what you want to talk about, you've got the wrong guy."

In-office measures like recycling are important, visible, and necessary. Aluminum cans, for example, are basically congealed electricity, since smelting aluminum from ore is so monumentally energy-intensive. But if progress stops at the trash-sorting station and the copy-machine paper, a lot of coastal copy machines are going to be under water.

Instead, businesses need to do some soul-searching to find their biggest lever, then use it. That lever isn't always obvious.

As I've pointed out before, the scope and scale of the climate problem makes some form of political action the biggest lever that any business or individual has. That's because, from a pure emissions standpoint, it's not enough for corporations to simply green up their operations. That is like rearranging deck chairs on the *Titanic*. We could, for example, eliminate all the greenhouse gas emissions in the ski industry, and we'd still go out of business in less than a hundred years if the rest of the world doesn't change. To get the government leadership we need, corporations must become involved in climate *policy* at the highest level possible.

But here is a key point: The on-the-ground work that is a focus of this book is a necessary precursor to that policy work. Why? Before businesses can effectively lobby for government action on climate, they need to have done something themselves or they lose their credibility and appear to be hypocrites. This may be the single most important reason businesses and individuals should implement carbon reduction: *So that their political case-making has more power and credibility*. In addition, there are, of course, large emissions reductions (and dollar savings) to be had while we wait for government leadership.

In turn, one way government can be forced to lead is by following the example of business. So how does a business determine the best way to address its own climate impact while supporting progressive legislation?

Think Like Wal-Mart, Not Ford

Wal-Mart is a good example. As it embarked on a greening program, the huge discount retail company could have done what the public would expect of such a company—in-store education, greening of individual sites, and little windmills and solar arrays that make a big statement but don't do much else. While Wal-Mart did do some of that, it also sat down and asked where its biggest impact was. As Charles Fishman wrote in *Fast Company* magazine:

> In the wake of Katrina, [CEO Lee] Scott had asked his staff for a briefing on environmental issues, including global warming. One of the people he sat down with was [Steven] Hamburg, the Brown professor who has won an award from the EPA for his ability to explain climate change.
>
> "It was a very frank conversation," says Hamburg. Not much of a Wal-Mart shopper, he had looked at one piece of Wal-Mart's environmental performance before. In 1994, he critiqued Wal-Mart's first environmentally sensitive store. "As I told Lee, it was a lot of greenwash.*
>
> He needed to do better. . . . I said, 'What really matters is what's on the shelves. Wal-Mart's influence is much greater in the marketplace than in the built environment.'"[1]

---

*Greenwashing is environmental tokenism. A full discussion of greenwashing can be found in Chapter 9.

Wal-Mart sells things, more things than any business in the world. So the way for Wal-Mart to change the world and protect the environment is through what it sells. As a result of this discussion, Wal-Mart set out to sell 100 million compact fluorescent bulbs, the efficient swirls that cut energy use by 75 percent, by marking the prices down and placing the bulbs at eye level in the aisle (prime selling space). Wal-Mart is creating a revolution by changing the market for bulbs. As of 2008, the company had sold 130 million bulbs (more than one for each American household), and the resulting pollution reduction through energy savings is the same as that of two large coal-fired power plants.

If the story ended there, it would be a great high-leverage story. But it continues. Wal-Mart isn't just selling a lot of compact fluorescents. *Wal-Mart is contributing to the extinction of the incandescent bulb.* Incandescents will be banned in Australia in 2010, and California is moving in the same direction.

Case studies of companies doing the opposite of what Wal-Mart did illustrate the need for a focus on what really matters. Ford, like Wal-Mart, sat down to ask, "What's our biggest lever?" The automaker made the colossal mistake of deciding not to green its core business (cars) but instead to throw $2 billion at greening its Rouge auto plant in Dearborn, Michigan. (In particular, they decided to install a green roof . . . planted with grasses.) Ford simply missed what its biggest lever was. As a result, almost a decade later, Ford is still not seen as green, doesn't have a green fleet, and is being pounded by companies like Toyota and Honda that asked the same question and answered it correctly. (And the roof leaks.)

The property management firm that wanted to green its offices with recycled paper needs to make the same assessment Wal-Mart did: What is our greatest area of leverage? For property managers, the opportunity is in . . . surprise . . . property management! As we'll learn in Chapter 8, buildings are responsible for close to half of all global greenhouse gas emissions. The property managers who called me were responsible for hundreds of millions of dollars in condos, private homes, and commercial space, and they might well be able to save money for their clients while protecting the environment. But their initial thinking about the meaning of "environmentalism" wasn't steering them in the right direction.

Aspen Skiing Company's Lever

One day I walked into the office of our then-CEO, Pat O'Donnell, in despair. (Again.) What are we doing? I asked him. The work we'd done—from improving building and snowmaking efficiency to making renewable energy purchases and using biofuels in Snowcats—was so small in the scheme of things; it felt like we weren't really making a difference. What was the point of this? Pat pointed out that while what we did day to day was important, it was dwarfed by another opportunity, and maybe we should consider that opportunity part of our on-the-ground work, too. Pat argued that an increasingly important part of our focus, now that we had credibility, should be changing the perspective of other businesses and supporting the burgeoning environmentalism of our ownership—a caring and generous family that was becoming increasingly environmentally aware.*

Aspen's biggest lever is the fact that it is world-renowned; as a result, we get covered by the press all over the world, and small action on our part can often influence disproportionate change. At Aspen Skiing Company, we felt that we could influence two huge entities with this thinking: the federal government and large corporations. And here's a crucial point: Our successful work on the ground gave us the credibility to lobby others for even bigger changes.

Leveraging Government

In an effort to pull the government lever, in 2007, at the request of friends at the Natural Resources Defense Council, Aspen Skiing Company filed an amicus (friend-of-the-court) brief to the Supreme Court on a lawsuit called *Massachusetts v. EPA*. That filing, which has been called the most important environmental lawsuit ever to go to the Supreme Court,

---

*Since that time, the family has spearheaded a dedicated effort throughout all their businesses to save energy, family members serve on the boards of the world's largest and most effective environmental NGOs, and they've launched a new philanthropic venture dedicated solely to the environment. At a recent remodel discussion at the Nell, a family member said, "You'll be doing this all in an environmentally responsible way, of course?" Aspen Skiing Company didn't make this change happen but was a part of the evolution.

demanded that the Environmental Protection Agency (EPA) regulate carbon dioxide as a pollutant under the Clean Air Act—something the plaintiffs saw as a very reasonable request since the Clean Air Act defines a pollutant as a substance that is damaging to humans. There is ample evidence now that CO_2 is already threatening human life.

At first glance, the participation of a ski resort—a small business by global standards—would seem to be meaningless. But because Aspen has such high name recognition, and because having a ski resort involved in the story is odd and unique, the press coverage looked something like this: "12 states, three environmental groups, even a *ski resort*, have weighed in in support of this lawsuit."[2] The suit won, 5–4.

I like to think of this approach as "asymmetric warfare" on Aspen Skiing Company's part: A small entity exerting disproportionate influence over a much larger, stronger entity. Aspen Skiing Company is a very small player in most environmental arenas. Our job is to find out how we can have a vastly disproportionate impact.

Several months later, when a Kansas review board denied a permit for a new coal-fired power plant, the basis of the denial was the future negative impact of the CO_2. It was the first time such a denial had been issued—and the only legal basis for that denial was *Massachusetts v. EPA*. That a ski resort could have had anything to do with such a monumental policy shift is humbling, and gratifying, to say the least. That's why we consider the filing of this amicus brief one of the most important things we've ever done as a company, including opening our doors in 1947.

The Technology Trap

The good news is that once individuals or corporations break into the legislative arena, opportunities abound and many of them even make money. Here are some examples of the kinds of change good policy makes possible:

- Changing obsolete transformers that step down high-voltage power to household levels could cost-effectively save 12 billion dishwasher-cycles of electricity annually, but government action is needed to specify and incentivize the installation of the most efficient models.[3]
- Recycling waste heat from factories (the heat that literally goes up the smokestack) and using it to generate clean power could produce 14 percent of the electric power the United States now uses.[4]
- Establishing revenue-neutral tax changes (like the idea Al Gore and others have had to eliminate the payroll tax and replace it with a pollution tax) not only is politically feasible (what voter wouldn't support elimination of the payroll tax?) but would create market mechanisms to drive down emissions; such action, however, requires legislation.
- Algae could be used to create ten thousand gallons of renewable biofuels per acre per year (conventional production through soy produces about fifty gallons), all while absorbing CO_2. But such technology—along with more efficient solar panels, techniques for sequestering

CO_2 from power plants, and other technologies—needs huge support and Iraq War–style investment, not the paltry few billion the U.S. government invests annually in such technology.

There are hundreds of examples like these, most making use of existing technology and all already being supported by private investors and hugely wealthy venture capitalists like Vinod Khosla and the firm Kleiner, Perkins, Caulfield, and Byers, among many, many others. But the expansion and development of the right technologies won't happen fast enough without government support—what Tom Friedman has called a World War II–scale effort on energy efficiency and renewables.

Some of this discussion might lead you to believe that if we just hang on long enough and invest appropriately, we'll solve the climate problem through technological innovation. The key point here is that new technology development isn't the lever; the lever is policy that allows for the *implementation* of existing technology.

A focus on technology development is actually one of the most prominent emerging ways to *delay* action on climate change, and it is being used widely on the national stage. Climate policy expert Joe Romm calls it "the technology trap": Using the mirage of new and better clean energy technology to stall, rather than foster, action on climate change. What's so dangerous about this trap is that it's based in a very wily approach promoted by Frank Luntz and other Republican strategists, who point out that focusing on technology is the best way to sound like you care about global warming without actually doing anything about it. The thinking has gained traction through the work of what Romm calls "climate delayers" like Bjorn Lomborg (who used to be a climate denier) and Ted Nordhaus and Michael Shellenberger.

Shellenberger, Nordhaus, and Lomborg believe that what's needed to solve the very real climate problem are "disruptive clean-energy technologies that achieve non-incremental breakthroughs in both price and performance."[5]

Joe Romm responded to that proposal on his blog:

> Uhh, no. Energy policy is my field, and I have talked to virtually all of the leading energy policy experts over the past few years. A few believe as S&N [Shellenberger and Nordhaus] do (mostly academics), but the majority do not—especially those who are actual energy practitioners or who have taken the time to educate themselves on climate science. Yes, they all want much higher funding for clean energy R&D—who doesn't??? (other than the phantom "pain-and-sacrifice-loving" environmentalists that only S&N seem to have met).
>
> But the energy practitioners know that meaningful breakthroughs rarely if ever happen in energy. I can say that with very high confidence since I ran the federal office responsible for doing the vast majority of the research into new carbon-free technologies.
>
> And those who have studied climate science understand that we simply have run out of time to pin much hope on

breakthroughs that may never come no matter how much money we spend on R&D. Developed country carbon emissions need to peak in the next decade (and developing country emissions soon thereafter) or we will ruin the planet for the next 50 generations no matter what technologies they have at their disposal. Put another way, if we can't stop catastrophic global warming with technologies that exist now or are already in the pipeline, we aren't going to stop catastrophic global warming.[6]

Joe isn't alone in his argument. Royal Dutch/Shell, one of the biggest oil companies in the world, has noted that "typically it has taken 25 years after commercial introduction for a primary energy form to obtain a 1 percent share of the global market."[7]

We know how much time we have to solve climate, and this time frame won't cut it.

Force the Leaders to Lead

Only government can implement existing technologies fast enough. So while corporations need to shoot all their efficiency and renewable energy bullets trying to reduce their own carbon footprint, it's most important that they use their own business as a club to batter legislators with advocacy, use their influence over customers to create a grassroots movement, and allocate advertising dollars to a climate campaign aimed at a broad audience. Individuals must do the same—with our votes, our pens, and our feet; we must literally storm the barricades in the same way we drove other social transformations like civil rights or America's exit from Vietnam. Yes, we should also screw in efficient lightbulbs, but without the delusion that such actions are enough. Or, as Bill McKibben says, "By all means, screw in that efficient light bulb, but then go screw in a new senator." And as my friend the writer Jules Older adds: " . . . and stop getting screwed by the old one."

Some of our problems—civil rights was one, health care is probably another—are just too big to be solved without government's help. In this sense, NASA's James Hansen agrees with Dick Cheney. Writing in the *New York Review of Books*, Hansen noted that a "call for people to reduce their CO_2 emissions, while appropriate, oversimplifies and diverts attention from the essential requirement: government leadership. Without such leadership and comprehensive economic policies, conservation of energy by individuals merely reduces demands for fuel, thus lowering prices and ultimately promoting the wasteful use of energy."[8]

Hansen's point is deceptive because it is both disempowering and empowering at the same time. What can individuals do? Perhaps reducing our own CO_2, on a planetary scale, isn't going to do much. But in the end, who is going to cause the government leadership to happen? Individuals.

At Aspen Skiing Company, as with any large business or even government entity, the leaders really don't get much direct communication from the public. If our CEO, Mike Kaplan, were to get a dozen handwritten letters from the public on a given issue, I can guarantee we'd have a high-level meeting on the subject within a week. Imagine if there were a street protest outside our building. Individuals can drive change; they always do, and they've done it before. We need to get out in the streets, we need to bring our letters to the post office, and we need to force the leaders to lead.

The Issue with Tissue

While government action is crucial, some businesses are so big that their programs have the impact of government policies. Therefore, it's important to crack the whip on other businesses as well.

In 2006, in response to a request from Forest Ethics, Aspen Skiing Company joined a Greenpeace-led boycott of Kimberly-Clark (K-C) paper products, including the legendary brand Kleenex. The concern about Kimberly-Clark was the company's use of paper and pulp from endangered ancient forests. Greenpeace's boycott, which had seven hundred participants as of 2007, was organized to force K-C to stop using fiber from endangered forests, to use fiber certified by the Forest Stewardship Council, and to increase dramatically the percentage of post-consumer recycled fiber in all of their tissue paper products, since Kleenex uses no post-consumer waste.

Aspen Skiing Company joined the boycott by switching our mountains, hotels, and restaurants away from K-C products. In the process, I made the mistake of talking to the press about it. The press had a field day dreaming up headlines like

"The Issue over Tissue" and "Kleenex Maker Not Sneezing at Skico's Concern." While the reporting was fair, local columnists went nuts. One wrote a column titled "Save the Planet, Eat a Booger," and closed with blistering sarcasm:

> The modern reality is that the louder a corporation blows its own recycled aluminum trumpet on environmental issues, the more offensive that profit-seeking organization likely is to our global well-being. Good for Skico to focus so much of their own internal marketing resources lately on letting the world know about this ecological travesty disguised as mucus absorption technology.[9]

While Aspen Skiing Company received some limited kudos for the action, many locals felt the move was hypocritical and flagrant greenwashing. Who were we to pick on another business when we had our own problems? Worse, the move was seen as an easy PR opportunity for Aspen Skiing Company, one that didn't require much in the way of change or effort on our part. Internally, when we floated the idea of changing the name of a famous Aspen ski trail from "Kleenex Corner" to something else, the old-timers were outraged. (The name stayed.) The bad press lingered for more than a year after the event, with columnists referencing it again and again. The boycott was widely seen as a PR disaster, at least locally, for the company.

And it was. But it was also something else: The Kimberly-Clark boycott was one of the most important and influential actions taken by Aspen Skiing Company that year.

Almost as soon as Aspen Skiing Company sent a letter to Kimberly-Clark's CEO announcing its participation in the boycott, our CEO Mike Kaplan received a letter in response from their CEO. In short order, K-C flew in a team of high-level managers (including senior vice president of environmental affairs Ken Strassner) to talk to us about K-C's work.

Why did they care? Aspen Skiing Company buys at most $30,000 worth of product each year, and K-C is a $32 billion company.

K-C cared for the same reason that businesses like Ralph Lauren, Prada, and Louis Vuitton insist on locating stores in Aspen even though they might not be profitable. Because of its profile and reputation, Aspen drives public opinion. And the town is newsworthy. Although a boycott might or might not have been news, Aspen's participation was.

This boycott, like our amicus brief filing, is another example of Aspen Skiing Company's leverage strategy in action. Once again, we were using the Aspen name to drive disproportionate change as a small company.

When K-C arrived to meet with us, I expressly told them that I didn't want to hear a dog-and-pony show about their environmental programs. I had read their materials online. What followed, unfortunately, was a dog-and-pony show on their environmental programs. And to be honest, those programs were impressive. In addition, showing their open-mindedness, the K-C team agreed to meet with NRDC and Greenpeace as a result of our meeting. Coming into the meeting, we had felt that the primary issue was their unwillingness to engage the environmental community, which was the primary differentiator between Kimberly-Clark and, say, Georgia Pacific. I asked them why they wouldn't at least hold discussions.

One of the executives replied, red-faced: "Greenpeace occupied our offices. Would you negotiate with people who had invaded your office?"

The answer is, of course, "Absolutely." How else are you going to get them out? Not engaging these groups is a move from the 1950s. But most modern corporations make it standard practice to engage. In fact, Aspen Skiing Company has a long-standing policy of engagement, going back to 1998, when then-CEO Pat O'Donnell told my predecessor Chris Lane to find our biggest enemies in the environmental community. "Who really hates us? Get me the list. I want to buy them lunch at the Little Nell four times a year." The point wasn't to buy these guys off (though as I often told the group, "This is probably the best food you dirtbags are going to have all year"). The point was to have conversations, to give nonprofit heads and government leaders a direct line to the CEO so that they could air their concerns directly and be heard, and so that we could use them as a free consulting group, testing ideas on them before releasing new programs.

To its credit, K-C did agree to meet with NRDC and Greenpeace. Unfortunately, the talks failed. But we're certain the talks will continue. In the end, what some had called Aspen Skiing Company's "craven act of greenwashing" leveraged a long-term, ongoing, and serious CEO-level conversation about K-C's business practices.

Businesses Can Incentivize Each Other to Go Green

The opportunities for a corporation to pull this kind of corporate lever are virtually limitless. When Aspen Skiing Company needed to buy $250,000 worth of new office furniture, we bid the project out to three companies. In our request for bids, we asked what they would provide; how much it would cost; and what their environmental programs were. The three bids came in around the same price. We did an analysis of the environmental programs at each of the businesses and then awarded the contract to the company doing the most progressive environmental work, a business called Herman Miller.

If the story ended there, it would be great. A corporation was rewarded, monetarily, for its green stance and encouraged to be even greener, purely from a profit motive. But the story continues. We got a note from one of the furniture makers that didn't win the bid. "We consider ourselves pretty green too. Why didn't we win?" We sent them our analysis. Now another business is incentivized to further green themselves—again, purely motivated by profit.

This story is about driving corporate change from the outside. But how do you do it from the inside? How do you sell sustainability to people, to businesses, and to government leaders?

SIX

Sustainable Sustainability: Creating Lasting Change

Every human is human.

—HAITIAN PROVERB

When you walk into a public bathroom, the door almost always swings in, meaning you don't have to touch the nasty, germ-infested handle—you can open the door like a waiter, with your foot or shoulder. On the way out, though, you can't avoid it. But that doesn't make sense. You want to be able to exit the bathroom with clean hands . . . and we don't want people with dirty hands contaminating the doorknob for everyone else.*

Why don't public bathroom doors have the handles on the *outside*?**

....

*And many don't wash their hands. See Nicholas Bakalar, "Many Don't Wash Hands After Using the Bathroom," *New York Times*, September 27, 2005.

**The problem with bathroom doors was brought to my attention by J. Baldwin, the industrial designer and writer, when we worked together at Rocky Mountain Institute.

The answer isn't complex. *We've always done it that way.* The status quo is the human condition, and it's as true for business practices as it is for restrooms. Therefore, a huge piece of the green revolution is going to be about selling sustainability, and then making sure it happens. Whether you're dealing with an Aspen homeowner, a property manager, a business leader, government, or your spouse, at some point you need to make the sustainability pitch to someone who's effectively "the boss." But that pitch is just the starting point. (Assuming you're not simply chased out of the room.) You need a broader plan for making your green program stick by selling its economic and PR benefits and then ensuring that your work is durable. The strategy I've used to launch a sustainability program and ensure its success is as follows:

1. *Do a sexy project:* To get leadership's attention.
2. *Make the economic pitch:* Based on that project, make the pure economic pitch for going green—it's profitable! In the process, you need to ditch all remnants of the 1970s environmental movement, in particular the sense that you're on some moral high ground.
3. *Cement the program:* Take steps to ensure that your sustainability work itself is sustainable. That is, can it make money for the company? If it doesn't make money, is there still value to the work? Does the marketing department recognize and quantify that value? Work to create long-term, structural support for your department, in particular employee and community

backing, so that when the recession hits, your department isn't the first to get cut. Help leadership recognize that pure economics isn't enough—you'll only get so far without an *ethical* mandate for change—and ideally get them to implement some sort of mission statement or guiding principles as well. A component of this cementing effort is befriending and engaging the grunts. After all, you're a grunt, too.

4. *Establish partnerships:* Work with government, non-profits, and foundations to find a way to "prime the pump" for climate protection by leveraging cash contributions and expertise for green programs that offer limited or no savings and therefore won't be financed internally, at least not initially. Partnerships help you get at the additional, more expensive carbon reductions we need to achieve.

5. *Hype your success:* There's nothing like good press and national awards to encourage management to do more. It also helps spread the movement. (This is the subject of Chapter 9.)

Of course, the strategy outlined above is the *theory*. Below, we'll look at what it looks like in the real world.

Set the Hook with a Sexy Project

At least on the pure emissions reduction front, the best way to start projects at a new corporation is to follow the ways of the drug dealer. Provide a little bit of your product free of charge; then once they're hooked, you have a long-term customer. In fact, the best approach to bringing such projects to a business is to make the projects happen first, under the radar, and then bring the incredibly successful results to management. For example, even though the Nell garage retrofit was monstrously difficult to pull off, the end result got people excited. We reached a point where the CFO started accepting any efficiency or renewables project with an ROI of 12 percent or better, about twenty percentage points lower than most corporate hurdle rates for such projects. He would accept this rate, however, because he understood that the savings were real and the end product was high-quality. (In addition, he found himself receiving public credit for supporting progressive environmental work. He might even have been asked to accept an award. These are not situations that bean counters often find themselves in, and the glory is intoxicating.)

This approach—hammer out a sexy, cost-saving project immediately before you have a comprehensive program—flies in the face of the conventional wisdom about corporate change. It's generally understood that you'll meet the very barriers we encountered at the Nell if you haven't prepped the company culture first. But I disagree. If you start by setting up a long cultural change program, you rapidly reach a point where people are asking what the enviro guy in the executive division is doing . . . what's he actually getting paid for? When you say, "We're laying the foundation for cultural change," to Donnie, he'll take another long drag on his Camel while looking at you through heavily lidded eyes.

As an aside, remember that what you think is sexy as a climate and energy geek may not be perceived as sexy by the people you interact with. Case in point: my friend, on the sly, and in a fit of green ambition, replaced all the down-lights in his kitchen with early-generation compact fluorescent lamps. The second his wife walked into the kitchen she made him take them out. In this case, not only was there a gap in sexiness perception, but perhaps my friend should have laid the groundwork a little better, maybe in the form of some flowers or a *candle*light conversation.

Still, at some point you do have to make a pitch to the wife or senior management to implement either broad-based sustainable business strategies or more focused energy and climate work, above and beyond the first sexy project.

Making the Pitch for Green Business Practices

The pitch has become universal and straightforward: a host of benefits are associated with sustainable business practices, starting with cost savings and ending with good PR. Some of this work may be difficult, but in the end there are some good reasons for it. Your business will be more efficient and therefore more competitive. There *is* payback, even if it's not always great. And we simply have to get after the climate challenge if we want to have a prayer of solving it.

The benefits and reasons in favor of implementing a broad green business approach are outlined below.

The Case for Sustainable Business

- Dollar savings from energy efficiency
- Risk reduction (for example, aqueous parts washers eliminate hazardous waste and therefore the need for regulation and potential fines)
- Improved community relations and easier project approvals
- Ethical obligation ("It's the right thing to do")
- Supporting ownership values
- Reduced legal liability
- Most other smart, well-managed businesses are doing it (GE, 3M, Toyota, Starbucks, Wal-Mart, FedEx, Kinko's, Staples, and so on)
- Worker attraction and retention (idealistic young kids who end up at ski resorts for a season are particularly eager to work for an ethical company)
- Strategic vision (for example, considering the impact of future carbon regulation on business, or how that regulation might affect things like travel, profit margins, and staff levels)
- Better product (green design tends to be good design)
- Better management (companies pursuing a sustainability agenda must accurately measure natural resource use, which reveals opportunities to reduce waste and improve efficiency)
- Market differentiation and brand positioning (going green offers a way to make your product stand out in a field of very similar offerings)

- Free PR and marketing—free articles about your business!

So what does this pitch look like in the real world, and what are the results?

Usually the pitch starts as a purely economic play on efficiency and money savings. That can be narrowed further to target only programs with a good return on investment; that ROI threshold can be set very, very high if necessary. Strategically, this isn't a bad way to get a foot in the door of a very cautious business.

Below is an actual e-mail sent by a businessman/ environmental manager to a management team, making the pitch for implementing profitable climate solutions. It's a good example of the kind of pitch I've been involved with over many years. Note that he's entirely focused on energy, carbon management, and high ROI. The memo has been edited to ensure anonymity, and only the key parts are included.

To:	Management Team
From:	Energy Hero
Subject:	Reducing Energy Use and Costs Across Business Units

To help structure the conversation during tomorrow's meeting, below is a set of options for moving forward.

Decisions Needed to Move Forward

To make the most progress in this area in the months and years ahead, senior management needs to clarify and agree on the goals of energy-related efforts, and those goals—and their importance—need to be articulated to the managers of each business unit.

The overarching intent appears to be cutting energy use to reduce both energy expenditures and the associated environmental impacts of business units. More specifically, the goal could be establishing energy use and carbon emissions baselines for wholly owned business units and reducing them significantly over the next one to three years.

By focusing initially on energy-saving measures with the highest financial return, there should be no need in the near term to choose measures that cost more than the savings they would generate. This is especially true in light of volatile, generally rising energy commodity prices.

There's little in the memo to disagree with, no matter where you're coming from—especially since it's suggested that the ROI threshold set by these efforts might be as high as 100 percent. But in more than a decade of sending out this kind of memo myself, or presenting the same information in person to managers in various capacities, I've seen a strikingly uniform response, which includes one or all of the following concerns:

- We're not interested in "going green." Hemp carpets and bamboo floors distract from our corporate mission, which is profit-centric.
- Environment and management are two separate issues; even energy efficiency and management are two

separate issues. Green initiatives are not part of my mandate—making widgets is—and because it is a distraction from my core job, it is not appropriate to push on managers.

- Efficiency is good, but it's something the markets are already taking care of.

Very often, managers who are told "energy" and "high ROI" instead hear "green." They hear "green" because they think that's what the conversation is about, given the messenger, who often has "environment" in his or her title. And this is a reasonable response given the history of environmentalism. This history encourages managers to pigeonhole the memo author instantly because of who he is and what the subject is. I'm guessing that many, when delivered a pitch on efficiency from an environmental officer, hear: "Patchouli. Birkenstocks. Hairy armpits. Street protestors telling you to abandon your car, take cold showers, shoot your television, and use bad lighting or none at all." Add a dose of perceived condescension and righteousness from the average enviro manager, and that can seem fully inappropriate for a corporate setting. These responses are understandable, but they miss what's on the table for discussion.

Many businesspeople say they don't want a "green" agenda to interfere with "management" as defined as driving profits. Fair enough. And yet the initiatives I have historically pitched were entirely profit-centric—almost ridiculously so! The problem is that they don't come off that way. (Maybe I should stop wearing all those beads and tie-dyes?)

An equally common response is to assert that most efficiency measures available would have already been taken because they're profitable, since the invisible hand of the market is designed to capture those opportunities. It's the joke Amory Lovins likes to tell about the economist walking with his granddaughter, who sees a $10,000 bill on the ground. The girl wants to pick it up, but the economist says: "Don't bother. If it were real, someone would have picked it up already." As we've seen already, there are many barriers and obstacles in business to capturing those savings, even if they represent $10,000 bills lying on the floor. There are in fact many very good reasons for not picking that bill up, not the least of which is that you might be able to pick up a $100,000 bill in the same movement by selling something you manufacture. (That's certainly what Eric Calderon was talking about at the Nell.) Historically, business itself has indeed been the moneymaker, not energy savings.

Still, one has to wonder why this miscommunication consistently occurs. Why do managers hear "hippie nonsense" when what was pitched was "moneymaking investment"? The short answer is that there is a hangover from the 1970s that continues to hamper the environmental movement today. That hangover affects modern attitudes about who environmentalists are and the attitudes they bring to the fight.

Preempting the 1970s Hangover

In a way, modern environmentalism, which is pragmatic, businesslike, collaborative, and climate-focused, has been hamstrung by historical environmentalism, which was often shrill, exclusionary, irrational, and microfocused. Being mis-characterized as a tree-hugger is something that makes my job, and the jobs of others in my field, much more challeng-ing than it would be otherwise. In 1997 I attended the first American intensive training in the "Natural Step" in Santa Fe. The Natural Step is a Swedish approach to sustainability. The meeting was filled with hard-core businesspeople, scien-tists, and some equally hard-core "environmentalists." At the end, one woman stood up and said, "I cry for the earth every day" and broke down in tears. It was horrifying to me. *Get this woman out of this room and out of the environmental movement,* I thought. If she got out in the world, she was going to make my job all that much harder because people would think all enviros were wackos like her. And clearly, to this day, many do.

Many smart and successful businesspeople have been turned off by the historical environmental movement. A good example is T. J. Rodgers, the president and CEO of Sil-icon Valley chip-maker Cypress Semiconductor Corporation and chairman of SunPower, one of the leading manufactur-ers of solar panels in the United States. Rodgers told *Fortune* magazine that "the group that is most vehement about global warming represents to me some of the worst people in the world. I dislike them so much it's difficult to listen to what they have to say objectively."[1] And yet this response is com-ing from a man who is doing more to develop renewables and energy efficiency technology than most people. He calls most environmentalists "coercive utopians" who want to force companies and individuals to do what they think is right for the earth.[2]

Rodgers argues that "environmentalism should be a science in which the collection of data and analysis of it dominates decision making. At this time, especially in government and university circles, I see environmentalism literally as a *secular religion* in which a set of beliefs that are not required to be supported by fact are used to tout the intellectual and moral superiority of a cult. . . . The ultimate state of enlightenment of members of the Church of the Holy Environment is to internalize that humans are evil and bad and that they only pollute and destroy things that are good, namely the environment."[3]

Ouch. Talk about a hangover from the seventies! In fact, the old environmental movement was very much as Rodgers describes it, and it's still alive and well in many circles. On a plane recently, a grandma from Ohio who was sitting next to me asked what I did. When I told her, she said: "Oh, you're an *environmentalist.*"

Thinking of the woman in tears hurting for the earth every day, I said, "Ah, no, uh . . . not really . . . I mean, not in the sense you mean, not with all the baggage that comes with the term." The grandma had flashed on exactly what the manager did: righteous, unwashed, and unshaven street protesters calling for a ban on business and radical cuts in the quality of your life, maybe even depopulation. I told the Ohio grandma that I really thought of myself as a businessman, nothing more. And yet, even in my business, people think of me as the environmental stereotype: the bearded old man living in the forest, the naturalist, the radical. I get called "tree-hugger" every day.

After my presentation to senior management when I put the COO, John Norton, on a bike, a manager came up to me and said: "Tell me about mountain lions. . . . I want to learn about mountain lions at the next meeting." I was dumbfounded. He might as well have asked me about post-Impressionist painting for all I knew about lions. But the perception of an environmental department's role was that it was established to educate management about things like mountain lions. If I wanted to succeed, I had to change that perception fast.

Ethics Have to Play a Role

The 1970s movement, which was based in large part on a moral foundation, wasn't wrong, but it was presented in such a strident and unappealing way that it turned off whole generations of businesspeople. In fact, there must be an ethical aspect to a corporation's sustainability work, because not every obstacle can be overcome with a return on investment. But instead of destructive "I'm better than you" or "you are evil" moralizing, I'm talking about ethics: simple, conservative values like honesty, respect, and care for the natural world. I'm talking about businesses having a sense of "the right thing to do."

As we saw above, an economic pitch in a vacuum may not make sense to managers if there's no context, no broader environmental mission within the company. Because of all the obstacles, if your only tool is an economic one, implementing sustainable practices in your business can either be impossible or lead to cream-skimming—only the most lucrative projects getting implemented and everything else getting rejected.

This is a real danger for corporations, and in fact it's probably the default setting. As I've discussed before, by undertaking several, even many, lucrative greening efforts, a business saves money and gets huge environmental kudos but never drills down deep enough to achieve the 80 or 90 percent CO_2 reductions that will have to happen if we want to solve the climate challenge.

And yet the pitch made by most sustainability NGOs to businesses is a purely economic one, so it virtually ensures this outcome. Coming from the nonprofit sector originally myself, this was how I approached the challenge at first.

Shortly after Aspen Skiing Company completed one of the first certified "green" buildings in the United States—the Sundeck Restaurant on Aspen Mountain—I was taking questions at a press conference with CEO Pat O'Donnell. Sticking to the green-building industry line—that environmentally responsible construction makes economic sense—I bent the truth and told the assembled reporters, "Many of the green elements in this building added no cost but improved the quality of the structure. Other measures cost more but offered rapid payback. Green construction is a sound investment because you get a better product at virtually no extra cost, with long-term health and financial benefits."

Pat's response was very different. "We did this because it was the right thing to do," he said. "It cost us hundreds of thousands of dollars more, but management and ownership agreed that this is part of our guiding principles and part of our values-based business." Pat's statement horrified me—it ran completely contrary to existing dogma in the sustainability movement, and it inserted ethics into what I believed, publicly at least, should be a purely economic argument. To mention added cost (even if there *was* added cost), I feared, could hurt the entire green-building movement. In fact, I thought it was probably better to lie about the extra cost or spin it away rather than mention it.

The worst part of it was that Pat was right.

You can't be a leader in the green business field without a moral mandate. Why? Because in the real world, most management teams will adopt a green approach only if it promises profits. And not every environmental action is profitable. To repeat: *If sustainability were cheap and easy, businesses would have achieved it by now.* The problem is that it's fundamentally difficult and often expensive. There isn't always a financial return on investment (despite what most consultants claim), and if there is, it may be so far out that it's unacceptable to many CFOs. Moreover, corporations, by definition, are singularly focused on profit and shareholder returns. Thus, environmental efforts that cost shareholder value in the short term (and they all do) often die in infancy. To preserve the ability to make ethical decisions, many sustainable business leaders have remained private, like Patagonia, or reverted to private ownership, like Levi Strauss.

In Chapter 3, we learned about the purely economic argument I made for the Nell retrofit. It never would have happened without a push from our CEO, who realized we had to do this for deeper reasons than ROI. Though that story unfolded on a small scale, the principles at work were as relevant to a multibillion-dollar corporation as to a ski resort.

On a larger scale, corporate America's experience with green energy illustrates how some of the most significant environmental measures offer no payback, at least at first glance. For most organizations, energy use is the largest component of their environmental footprint. Thus, an initiative like purchasing wind power is one of the most visible statements any business can make about its environmental commitment. But you can't make an economic argument for it—it simply costs more, especially if you are buying wind credits, not direct power, which most businesses do. Guiding most of the early corporate wind credit purchases was an aggressive commitment to environmentally sound business. The environmentally minded companies have been willing to pay more. This was before it became clear that wind energy purchases provided ample return on investment in public relations—a realization that corrupted the clean power industry and created the partially fraudulent renewable energy credit business (see chapter 7 for a detailed discussion). Nonetheless, those businesses had to get outside the ROI box, and ethics is what lives outside that box.

The bottom line is this: Corporate sustainability won't occur without a company mandate that springs from ethics rather than from economics. Economics will get you part of the way there, but it will leave you hanging far from the finish line.

When the Sales Pitch Fails

Ethics aside, sometimes you have to "win ugly." Or, as Al Davis of the Oakland Raiders is famous for saying, sometimes you have to "just win, baby." It doesn't matter how. Often the only way to overcome cultural resistance is to wait for the person in charge to go away, whether by leaving the company, getting fired, retiring, or dying.

That was the case when we tried to change our trail maps and marketing materials from a virgin paper product to something with postconsumer recycled content, like what this book is printed on. It seemed deeply hypocritical to make any claims as a green business but to keep printing most of our marketing materials—hundreds of thousands of printed units—on virgin paper. By printing on high levels of postconsumer waste, we could turn a bad—printing a bunch of stuff that ultimately becomes garbage after using up loads of energy—into a good: by buying the postconsumer paper, we'd be supporting a market for recycled product waste.

But when I proposed this to our marketing manager at the time, she said simply:

"No."

Recycled paper, she said, looks dirty and grimy. Worse, if you make trail maps out of it, when the maps get wet "they get all crinkly. And anyway—this is *Aspen*. We print beautiful, glossy brochures. We don't do recycled paper. We don't want our stuff to look like brown paper bags from the supermarket." I knew at the time that this was absurd. The crinkliness of recycled paper was as much a figment of her imagination as the notion that fluorescent bulbs don't save energy. But her personality was such that she wouldn't budge. My solution? Nothing artful, profit-realizing, glorious, or even intelligent. I waited for her to leave the company, then tried again. She was replaced, and her position was filled over time by two different women with open minds (and husbands who were my occasional drinking buddies). Now Aspen Skiing Company prints on 100 percent postconsumer waste. The marketing materials are clear, clean, and beautiful, and the trail maps don't get crinkly in the snow.

The Ripple Effect

Even recycled paper represents a "new technology," and a reality is that the chance of getting burned by new things is omnipresent in business. To wit: waterless urinals.

It seemed like a good idea to me. In 2000 the waterless urinal was a relatively new technology, but one with great promise. It presented a rare opportunity to cut water use to zero in an appliance, with no change in service. After all, I asked when presenting the idea to senior management, "Who flushes a urinal anyway?" (Eric Calderon, my friend and the general manager of the little Nell, responded, "I do. My parents raised me properly.")

Using water efficiently is a huge and growing component of the sustainability puzzle. And it's also a piece of the adaptation component of climate change—since there's warming already in the system, which almost guarantees water shortages, part of our climate strategy must focus on adaptation.

Surprisingly, it's very difficult to do better than business as usual for most appliances; since the Energy Policy Act of 1992, all new toilets, urinals, and showerheads have had to meet strict efficiency requirements. (Keep this in mind when you hear people bragging about their buildings being green because they have "low-flow" or "high-efficiency" fixtures: Often they were merely complying with the law when they installed them.)

We decided to try a waterless urinal at the Snowmass Club. I bought the best one on the market, and our maintenance staff installed it. If it worked out, we'd switch the entire company.

Our CEO at that time, Pat O'Donnell, did his morning workout at the Snowmass Club, starting at around 5:00 AM with an hour of hard cardio, then moving into the weights. So he'd be one of the first to see, and perhaps test out, the urinal.

Early one morning as I arrived at work, Pat flagged me down through the window of his office.

"Auden," he said. "I was doing my workout this morning, and I took a piss in the waterless urinal."

"Oh?" I said.

"Yes. It stank. And there was a fossilized residue in the bottom that was disgusting. I'm going on vacation next week, and when I come back, I want that thing gone."

We pulled the urinal out. No big deal, right? We'll try another one, or technology will improve and we'll move to that new, better product. After all, this technology had just been invented.

Wrong. It *was* a big deal.

After a little while, I suggested to some maintenance staff that we try another model. Pat got wind of this idea and said, "Over my dead body." In fact, he swore that we'd never use waterless urinals during his tenure. *This was coming from the company's environmental visionary, the man who started our programs in the first place.* If that wasn't bad enough, the concept of the waterless urinal became a big company joke. As in: "Hey, Auden, got any other brilliant projects for us lately? Something like a waterless urinal?"

Today waterless urinals are used widely—even at other ski resorts like Alta and Snowbird—with no smell or "fossilized residue." In fact, the Washington Intercontinental, a four-diamond hotel that was voted the best in Washington, D.C., and ranked one of the top five hundred hotels in the world by *Travel + Leisure* magazine, has these urinals in its public areas. This hotel even won the Best Bathroom Award in 2006 from *Executive Traveler*. But more than five years after our first experiment, we're still flushing urinals at the Snowmass Club.

The lesson here is that if you're an early adopter of new technology and the project doesn't work, you've been burned for all future projects. A green project can actually make you less green in the long run if project managers later refuse to take a "risk" on a similar project, even when there is no risk, only the perception of risk. This ripple effect is something to avoid if possible. As the urinals showed, we weren't always so lucky.

The point of this story is to show that, in every case, we have the technology to solve the problem. The challenges are always human, either behavioral or cultural. The art and science of solving climate change, then, is analyzing these barriers and finding ways around them.

So how do you get around these human barriers?

You've Got to Be Tough

We had another opportunity to do a large garage lighting project on the scale of the Nell—this time from scratch—in an eight-hundred-unit underground garage planned in Snowmass Village. When I suggested during the design phase that we use the efficient type of lighting installed at the Nell, the engineers we had hired came up with a reason for not using it that I hadn't heard yet.

"There was a garage in Oakland where someone used a baseball bat to knock out those fixtures. Then the guy attacked someone."

"Hmmm . . . Snowmass isn't exactly Oakland, but couldn't you use a bat to knock out *any* kind of fixture?"

"Well . . . yes. But you still don't want to use that kind of fixture. You can't pressure-wash the ceiling of the garage if you use it."

"In human history, has anyone ever pressure-washed the ceiling of a garage?"

"No."

This exchange was an "Aha!" moment for me. These guys didn't want to use different lights. Period. It had nothing to do with anything other than not wanting to change.

There are no silver bullets to help you get past this sort of resistance other than grit, doggedness, and determination. But that realization in itself is enlightened thinking. Why? Because nothing in your training, nothing in the literature, nothing the consultants or the government agencies tells you about sustainability says, "You have to be tough—you have to be a bulldog." You'll never hear a consultant say, "There's no way around this—you have to beat those guys down with a lead pipe or outlast them. Bring a football helmet and a battle ax." But it's true.

That's why the best advocate for any given project resembles Dog the Bounty Hunter more than Mr. Science. For me, the role model for winning these battles (and we did win this one—there are superefficient ceramic metal halide fixtures in this garage now) is Jimmy Connors in the 1983 U.S. Open. He won that championship even though diarrhea forced him to leave the court several times to go to a bathroom. "It wasn't quite as beautiful as some other finals I have played," Connors told Ross Atkin of the *Christian Science Monitor* in September 1983. "And maybe wasn't the best match to look at, but it got the job done."

That's the kind of grit you need. The technology exists, and what's missing is the will.

To find the will, sometimes you need a melon launcher.

Befriending the Grunts . . .
with a Melon Launcher

If you can sell to senior management but not the ground troops, you're as dead in the water as if you hadn't started. So how do you make the pitch on the trench level? As with most of our environmental projects at Aspen Skiing Company, the idea for using biodiesel in our snowcats came from a guy on the front lines. In this case it was Lyle Oliver, a thirty-year veteran of our snowmaking department. Lyle was gruff, old, no-nonsense, and wore his Levis beltless, hanging down over his hips. One day he came up to me and said: "If you were as 'green' as you think you are, you'd be using this." And he handed me a *Denver Post* article on something called biodiesel.

I looked into it. Biodiesel is diesel—it works just the same as regular diesel fuel—but it's made from agricultural crops like soybean and canola. In Aspen, air quality is a huge issue. While our measurements show that on the top of Aspen Mountain the air is some of the cleanest in the United States, down in the valley where diesel buses, trucks, and snowcats work overtime, our air quality for years hadn't been in compliance with even minimum EPA standards.

When we looked at our total environmental impact as a resort, we realized that we burned 260,000 gallons of diesel each year, most of it in snowcats, and that was contributing to local air quality problems.

You can't buy a radically more fuel-efficient snowcat the way you can buy a hybrid car—the best you can do is buy the most current models on the market. So in the absence of an efficiency option, we decided to target fuel. That took me into the room with vehicle mechanics, again.

The scene is the same. I'm in a starched shirt, and they're in dirty overalls or Carhartt pants. All of the lead mechanics are named Don. It's a generational thing. I call them "the Dons." I know very little about snowcats, and they know a good deal about not just snowcats but all things mechanical.

When I come in and propose using French fry grease in snowcats (you can also make biodiesel from French fry grease), they see me as Pee Wee Herman—an annoying freak who is clueless about what they do. And I see them as Mr. T, with his best look of skepticism—angry, closed-minded, and inflexible. Their first response, predictably, is "No."

There is a trust problem between the frontline workers in any corporation and the brass, the white-collar managers. That lack of trust often comes from the blue-collar/white-collar divide, which itself results from the fact that people don't hang out together. These guys don't really know each other. A problem is that management will understand the theory and direction behind much of the work that has to get done, but only the guys in the shop know how to make it happen. There's a potential impasse there, and getting beyond it—once again, addressing culture, not technology—is absolutely vital if we hope to move forward. It's also crucial to understand the nature of the divide so that we can solve it.

It would be easy to stereotype the mechanics. They're uneducated, ignorant. They don't care about the environment because they're stupid. This is the knee-jerk opinion of many environmentalists when other people don't seem to get where they're coming from. But let's dig a little deeper.

Far from being ignorant or uneducated, ASC's snowcat mechanics are smart and skilled. They have decades of experience working on snowcats and vehicles, and they know what works and what doesn't. Since each snowcat costs a quarter of a million dollars, and since downtime represents a ski run that's not getting groomed—and therefore a guest who's not happy—it's paramount that the cats stay up and running. There's no incentive for mechanics to try something new, because they know what works. If they'd gotten in the habit of saying yes to every idea proposed by the new enviro "college boy" who walks in the shop, they'd have lost their jobs long ago. Here's the scenario they might imagine with regard to biodiesel:

"Auden, we put that French fry oil in our cats, and they broke down. My whole fleet of $250,000 cats broke down. We weren't able to groom the slopes last night, which means my boss got mad at me because customers were angry. Lots of guests were unhappy. And I had to get up at 3:00 AM to work on our equipment. It was minus-twenty out."

"Hmmmm, Donnie, that's really unfortunate. But gosh, I'm not a mechanic, I studied biology. I don't think I can help you here. . . . I'm really sorry!"

Now, let's imagine that Donnie has other issues in his life other than a green crusade—for example, might he have a crushing mortgage (very likely in and around Aspen) or a child in college? Perhaps he also has a sick family member, residual debt, or who knows what else. When Donnie does what's right in his mind to protect the company and his job, he's not being a green skeptic, he's being a realist and a good employee.

Still, biodiesel was a good idea. The issue wasn't biodiesel, it was trust. How could I break down the blue-collar/white-collar divide here and get inside the trust circle of the cat mechanics?

Walking around the shop one day, checking on the hazardous waste storage site, or maybe looking longingly at a new aqueous parts washer (how cool!), I saw something out of the corner of my eye. It looked like a giant crossbow, the size of a car, complete with a cut metal Aspen leaf logo ornament.

I casually asked Donnie about it.

"Oh, that's our melon launcher. Every year at the end of the season we go to the annual ski area vehicle mechanic conference in Grand Junction. On the last day we go out into a big field and eat a bunch of barbecued pork, and then we see who can huck a melon the farthest. The rules are you can't use compressed air—just springs and tensioned metal."

I took a picture of the launcher.

The next day I walked past Pat O'Donnell's office at about eight in the morning. At that point Pat has already been up for three hours, working out for most of that time. I took the picture of the melon launcher and put it up against the glass. Pat looked and waved me in.

"What the hell is that?" Like most guys' guys, Pat was fascinated by militaristic-looking things: artillery, pumpkin chuckers, big slingshots.

"A melon launcher. It will send a Green River cantaloupe 250 yards. Each year our vehicle shops build these things and compete against other ski resorts. Last year Breckenridge beat us."

Pat stood up. "We've got to go beat those guys next year. We've got to win."

The result was a full-court press on the R&D of a better, bigger, stronger melon launcher. Every day now the shop was in the huge parking lot outside our administration building, hucking melons. Dozens of hours of shop time were dedicated to the machine. No expense was spared.

In the end, they built a mechanical arm, on the end of which the mechanics would place a cantaloupe. In several tests, the launcher was so strong, and the melon so soft, that the "ammo" simply evaporated in place when they pulled the trigger. We lost the competition to Breckenridge again, and later in the summer Pat called a halt to the R&D, since it was taking over other shop responsibilities.

But the result of the quest for a better melon launcher was that we became, if not friends, then at least more human to each other. Some level of trust evolved. I realized that these guys weren't ignorant or stubborn; they realized that I wasn't a head-in-the-clouds, know-nothing, idealistic college boy (at least not entirely). The end result—which came after Lyle Oliver, who first suggested biodiesel, grumpily retired—was that we switched to a blend of 20 percent biodiesel in all our snowcats. We did it slowly—first with a test batch at our smallest mountain, then a year later on top of Aspen Mountain where it gets cold and we could test concerns about the fuel gelling in the cold, and then later on all our mountains.

It hasn't been a flawless product—we've had clogged filters and microbial growth in fuel tanks—but we've worked out the problems, and other resorts and the local transit agency have followed our lead. The company and the mechanics eventually arrived at agreement on the issue, and some of the crustiest cat drivers even came to joke about it.*

Recently, one of those drivers, Mark Gressett, who favors T-shirts with the sleeves cut off and usually dines on peanut M&Ms and Mountain Dew, greeted me at a preseason ski sale. Gressett can curse like no one I've ever met. With little provocation, he's able to unleash a salvo of unbelievably offensive expletives, most involving your mother, strung together with what can only be described as an artistic sensibility. He's also an artist with a track hoe, one of the best "operators" in the country, and a perennial winner of snowcat precision grooming competitions. I've seen him move rocks

....

*ASC got lots of good PR for the biodiesel. But in 2008 two things happened. First, new federal regulations kicked in, requiring that all diesel meet strict new pollution standards. The cleaner diesel negated the benefits of biodiesel. Next, the biofuels craze caused the price of biodiesel to spike; simultaneously, new research showed that biodiesel might not be so good for the planet. No longer seeing any clear benefit to the product, we stopped using it. So it goes.

the size of baseballs with a single tooth on a multiton track hoe. Gressett came up to me, put his hand on my shoulder, and said, "Ahhh, Auden, I spent the summer burning a lot of that number-one diesel. God, I love that number-one diesel." (Number 1, the highest-grade, most expensive diesel, is decidedly not biodiesel.)

I looked down and saw his other hand, with middle finger extended, pointing up at my face. He smelled vaguely of diesel, as he always does. I looked back at his eyes, all crinkled up and twinkling mischievously.

And there he was: squeezing my shoulder, flipping me off, and grinning. This guy had become my friend.

Making Sustainable Business Practices Durable

One of the hardest parts of selling sustainable business practices to management (and staff) is that the programs are typically seen as a cost center to the company. And therefore one of the least sustainable aspects of a corporate sustainability effort is that the department in charge—or the program itself— is usually the first to get cut in times of economic downturn, or even as a result of changes in leadership in the business.

Unfortunately, environmentalism has always been seen as a luxury, something we can do if we have the money. In my tenure at Aspen Skiing Company, I've seen these positions get eliminated (sometimes to be reinstated) at L.L. Bean, Nordstrom, and Birkenstock, among others, typically for financial reasons.

How can sustainability be sustainable if it's always in danger of being cut—if not now, then in a few years? At Aspen Skiing Company, we began receiving numerous calls asking for help, advice, and guidance. We realized that we couldn't respond to these requests and still do our job, but it was clear that there was a niche for sustainability consultants who had experience on the ground. We started a consulting business to respond to these requests. Our thinking was that if the environmental department—typically seen as a burden on the company—became a profit center, then that division—and sustainable practices within the company—would really become sustainable.

Ironically, this new business arm—and new source of revenue—is in itself a hedge against climate change. If skiing is gone one hundred years from now, perhaps we should grow this department—and our experience and expertise—so that by the time the snow-based business model is done, we're a full-fledged McKinsey and Company–sized environmental consultancy with the odd name, in 2100, of "Aspen Skiing Company." As skiing becomes less viable, perhaps giving advice on how to avoid this industry's fate becomes *more* viable.

This approach isn't unique. At the same time Aspen Skiing Company's environmental department created its consultancy, Jim Hartzfeld at Interface, the floor-covering manufacturer that is perhaps the leading corporate implementer of sustainable practices, started one there. Jim has gone from very busy to ridiculously busy. While his goal was to share information, make money, and spread the sustainability movement, his work also makes his division indispensable to the business. Interface will probably always make carpet, but don't be surprised if it becomes better known for its consulting.

Becoming a profit center is just one of many ways to ensure the sustainability of a company's environmental department. In Aspen, I think you could fairly argue that our environmental programs are so popular among employees (who are proud of them) and the community (many of whom find them fun, inspirational, and hopeful) that cutting these programs would be impossible. The community and employee outrage would be overwhelming.

Whether green work is justified by profit, savings, PR, or ethics, the key is that it ends up being seen as something more than a "nice to have." It must be perceived as invaluable, because it is.

Priming the Pump for Efficiency

Aristotle thought that we become virtuous by *practicing* virtue.[4] The philosopher Peter Singer uses blood donors as an illustration of this principle. Based on a study at the University of Toronto, researchers showed that initial donations are typically inspired by an external event, like a friend's urging. Subsequent donations, however, are increasingly driven by a sense of social responsibility or moral obligation. At some point, the action becomes habit: "I've always done this." Humans work that way: they develop habits, and those habits are hard to break. Sometimes it takes an external event to "prime the pump."

I think there's a lesson here for driving corporate action on climate change. If we could make emissions reduction the habit—or better yet, addiction—of business, we'd be on our way to solving the climate problem. But how do you do it? Many nonprofit organizations are already trying, with limited success. Given the scale and longevity of energy infrastructure and the expected rates of economic and population growth, the climate challenge is the equivalent of a five-alarm fire. But as I said earlier, we're all like fish in water, and corporations are no exception: though they swim in energy, they don't see it, or the potential for savings and associated emissions reductions.

The problem with most NGO or government greenhouse gas emissions reduction programs for business is that they're designed around providing technical support—how-to information—then letting the business run with the ball. They also rely on the coercion associated with voluntary commitments or membership.

The World Wildlife Fund Climate Savers Program and the Pew Center on Global Climate Change, for example, provide businesses and municipalities with knowledge, background, peer networks, and studies. The problem is that most businesses already know climate change is a problem, and they know what they need to do about it. Running yet another study showing that retrofitting compressors has climate benefits and a five-year return on investment is not news, though commissioning the study may make a business (or nonprofit) look good.

Partners in the EPA's Climate Leaders Program "set aggressive corporate-wide greenhouse gas reduction goals, and inventory their greenhouse gas emissions to track progress toward their reduction goals." Everyone and their brother is doing a greenhouse gas inventory these days. But we have to act now, coupling *action* with inventories, or we're going to be hosting a lot of Dutch and Bangladeshi neighbors in our guest rooms.

There's a strong case for action, of course. Amory Lovins says we're missing $300 billion in energy savings and emissions reductions in the U.S. economy alone, all with reasonable return on investment. Whether you agree with that number or not, the consensus is that the opportunities for savings are large and real. We've seen how inaction results from a host of obstacles, from first-cost barriers to a lack of understanding of the benefits of energy efficiency.

The accepted way to overcome these barriers and introduce business to emissions reduction is to create a global carbon-trading market by putting a price on CO_2 emissions. This would provide larger ROIs than exist from energy savings alone, and it would also create a profession and core competencies in emissions reduction.

This is correct thinking, and it's why almost everyone in the climate field—from government to environmental groups, from left to right—has hung their hopes on carbon trading to save the world. We have enormous faith in the market's ability to solve problems, if it's sending the right signals. But there are two short-term problems. Even if we successfully created a global market, it would be a new practice: businesses would need training wheels to navigate the new trading landscape. Second, most economists think that, to be successful and economically palatable, the initial carbon price has to be low and rise over time. That's because successful climate policy must be enduring policy, to be enduring it must be bipartisan, to be bipartisan it must be gradual, and to be gradual a carbon price must start low. That means a carbon price would be a weak signal initially.

In short, a carbon market, with prices in the range that are politically feasible, is not going to change the fact that energy remains remarkably cheap. But we need to wring carbon out of the economy *now*. So the question becomes: how do we teach corporations something they've never done before, then make it a habit?

The Chicago Climate Exchange is trying to do this through a voluntary emissions trading program. Right now the price is under a penny per pound, and not much trading is occurring. The bottom line: lots of carbon can be saved inexpensively, but we need mechanisms for getting people started. A carbon market could be the right solution, but we need to build a bridge to it in the short term.* One approach might be to use something corporations understand very well: cash.

....

*A carbon tax would probably be a better solution, since with carbon accounting there is all kinds of room for shuck and jive. But taxes are generally understood to be political unviable.

It often takes an initial cash infusion to overcome first costs and create an understanding of what energy efficiency and emissions reduction mean on the ground. A good example was the Little Nell garage lighting retrofit, which ultimately required a grant from a local nonprofit for one-quarter of the initial investment required. The grant was a big piece of what made the project possible.

It took a gift of money to a for-profit corporation, for a project with huge ROI—a suspect idea indeed—to teach management about the benefits of efficiency projects. But here's what came of it: now, when we propose similar projects with a 12 percent ROI or higher, our finance department typically says yes without blinking. We've primed the pump, and the emissions reduction tap is running, with no need for further cash input.

Another example: corporations can easily reduce emissions through *commissioning*—a third-party design review of the heating and cooling system in new buildings, followed by an inspection after installation to see if it's running properly. (You can do similar work in existing buildings. It's called retrocommissioning, and it's more or less the same work I did weatherizing old trailers.) Commissioning always leads to energy savings (and therefore return on investment and emissions reduction) because all heating systems are overengineered, and none run properly when first installed. (It's no sweat for a mechanical engineer to add an extra boiler—you'll never run out of heat, and you'll never complain!) Commissioning is a relatively new idea, with an upfront cost, but the benefits are so great that, once hooked, a business will continue the practice forever.

As an experiment with commissioning, Aspen Skiing Company hired an engineer to review plans for a heating and cooling system in a new building. The engineer pointed out that we had an extra heat pump—a large, expensive piece of equipment that was unnecessary in the design. When we removed it on his advice, we saved $10,000 instantly, covering the consulting engineer's fee and reducing the lifetime energy use and associated emissions of the building. And the commissioning agent hadn't even begun his job of inspecting the heating system once the building was built—which provides an opportunity for even more savings. Afterward, our managers said they'd commission all future buildings, and they've been true to their word.

While we didn't need to be persuaded to try commissioning because we're already in the habit of reducing emissions, most businesses do need a boost. It's an unanticipated upfront cost. Unfortunately, most nonprofits working on climate change are reluctant to give handouts. After all, why would anyone make a donation to a for-profit enterprise? But business—given its size and influence—is essential to addressing climate change. Isn't it worth a small investment to change how a business operates forever?

We need to find and drive new and different emissions reduction projects with big bang for the buck, and the best way to do this might be to create a climate action trust. Funded by a combination of government and private-sector foundation money, the trust would solicit proposals for emissions reduction that represented more than business-as-usual upgrades. Oregon's Energy Trust (www.energytrust.org), funded by a state public purpose tax on utility rates, is one such approach. But most states find it difficult to pass an energy tax, and the climate shouldn't suffer for lack of political will. A private, national version of Oregon's program funded mostly by foundations would circumvent tax-phobia but achieve the same goals. In effect, the climate trust would be an early market for carbon, since the trust would buy energy efficiency. (The trust would actually buy emissions reductions at a discount, because it would pay for only a portion of projects—just enough to overcome first-cost thresholds.)

The largest environmental groups in the world—the biggest has a budget of about $100 million—were originally founded to protect land and biodiversity. But both will be threatened or destroyed by climate change. Shouldn't the largest environmental group in the world be one that works on the largest environmental problem in the world? With $100 million annually, a climate trust could create a sea change in business. Even those companies that didn't receive grants would be driven to think about creative ways to cut energy use, because they'd be pursuing the free money.

A private climate trust could serve an educational role as well. After selecting cream-of-the-crop proposals for partial funding, the trust could partner with MBA classes to track the projects and write case studies. The result would be high-profile, innovative, replicable, documented, cost-effective emissions reductions on the ground, plus a new generation of climate protection specialists.

To stabilize atmospheric concentrations of CO_2, anthropogenic carbon emissions must approach zero by century's end. We need to get corporations in the habit of reducing emissions now so that when carbon trading matures, businesses will be addicted. And the way to get them addicted is to give them a free taste of the nectar of sustainable business practices.

We just have to make sure they get addicted to the good practices, not the phony ones.

SEVEN

Green Energy: The Key to Solving Climate Change (and Sometimes a Scam)

> We are compounded of dust and the light of a star.
>
> —LOREN EISELEY, *THE FIRMAMENT OF TIME*, 1960

reen energy is in many ways the philosopher's stone of climate change mitigation. It encompasses everything, from transportation and waste to water and agriculture. If we're going to solve the climate problem as a society and reduce our greenhouse footprint as businesses, we're going to have to create renewable energy *supply*. The world simply needs energy to operate, that need is growing inexorably, and even with radical efficiency we're going to continue to require a huge amount of power to run the planet. (The Energy Information Administration predicted in 2008 that world energy demand would increase 50 percent [!!!] by 2030 under business-as-usual conditions.)[1] Solve energy by making it clean, and you solve climate. And as we saw earlier, you solve a whole lot of other issues, too.

Energy Efficiency: The Promise and the Challenge

Here's a funny truth: by far the cheapest new source of energy supply isn't supply. It's energy *savings*, also known as energy efficiency, or what Amory Lovins calls "negawatts." In short, energy saved through efficient lightbulbs, pumps, and motors, good building design, and refined industrial processes provides utilities with more available capacity for others who need it. So instead of building a new coal plant, many utilities can (and do) try to save energy first by distributing efficient technologies, assisting businesses with big efficiency retrofits, and helping homeowners use less power. This makes sense—a so-called demand-side management program might cost a few million dollars, but a new power plant might cost a few billion. It costs much less per unit of energy to save electricity (to generate negawatts) than to make it from fuel. For example, California has been saving energy for years at a cost of between two and three cents per kilowatt-hour, which is the energy it takes to run your dishwasher through one cycle. To generate that amount of electricity from new nuclear power, which many see as a solution to climate change, would cost between fifteen and seventeen cents. In fact, negawatts come in at about one-fifth the price of power derived from new coal, natural gas, and nuclear plants combined. Why would you spend money on generating expensive power when you could find five times as much energy for the same price through efficiency? It would be fiscally imprudent to do anything else. Amory Lovins likes to think of it as drilling for cheap energy in your buildings and factories instead of in the ground or offshore.

Unfortunately, as we've seen, it's very easy to attain *some* efficiency cheaply, but much harder to get at the large cuts we need to achieve. And there are many complex twists to the energy efficiency path that can be exploited to create public confusion. Policy direction will be essential to providing clarity and ensuring success.

One idea pushed by the climate delayers is called Jevon's paradox, which states that as technological improvements make resource use more efficient, total consumption of that resource may increase rather than decrease.* Jevon's paradox at first appears to be simple economics, since more efficient use of a resource means that resource is essentially cheaper. (If it only costs a few cents to drive to the supermarket in your new Prius, you might be inclined to drive more often than you'd walk.)

Used as evidence for this paradox is a 2007 study by CIBC World Markets, which showed that American consumers are driving bigger, gas-guzzling cars and buying more air conditioners and refrigerators as the overall energy efficiency of products improves. Jeff Rubin, CIBC's chief economist and strategist, said: "While seemingly perverse, improvements in energy efficiency result in more of the good being consumed—not less." Rubin argues that customers

---

*After English economist William Stanley Jevons, who in 1865 observed that England's consumption of coal soared after James Watt introduced his coal-fired steam engine, which radically improved the efficiency of an earlier design.

use cost savings from greater efficiency to buy more and bigger stuff with it.

This makes energy analyst Joe Romm furious. In his blog, he writes: "First, there is no evidence whatsoever that consumers take money saved from energy efficiency and spend it on more and bigger appliances and vehicles. What has happened is that U.S. consumers have gotten considerably wealthier over the years, so they buy more stuff and bigger houses/cars—that is the well-known wealth effect and has nothing whatsoever to do with efficiency. There *is* something called the rebound effect, where the lower per-mile cost of a fuel-efficient vehicle in theory causes people to drive it more (although in statistical studies it is very hard to separate that out from the wealth effect). But the rebound effect is only at most 20%, and probably much less, possibly 10%. The best evidence that this study is utterly wrong is the fact that the state of California has kept per capita electricity consumption flat for three decades with aggressive energy efficiency."

There are other reasons to doubt Jevon's paradox. As Mike Brylawski, vice president of Rocky Mountain Institute's Transportation Practice, points out, studies show that Prius drivers in certain markets drive 40 percent less than other drivers. This is the opposite of what Jevon's paradox suggests. Why is that the case? In part, Prius drivers immediately become acutely aware of their impact because of the instantaneous miles-per-gallon readout on their dashboard. (This awareness can also make them pompous. The television cartoon *South Park* has a famous episode in which Prius drivers emit "smug," not smog.) Prius drivers start paying attention to how they drive (because when you floor it you see the miles-per-gallon plummet), and that awareness leads them to ask why they drive. Brylawski points out that in 2007 the Prius outsold every single American-made SUV in the U.S. market.

Policy Leadership Is Key

Given the complexity of implementing efficiency—both the difficulties we run into when we try to pull it off and the popular confusion about its success described here—it's clear that we need leadership from somewhere to navigate this tangled thicket. And it's not clear where that leadership would come from if not the government. The good news is that sensible government policy works! Mike Brylawski notes, for instance, that congestion pricing in London has cut vehicle miles traveled by 20 percent. A government program that tapped the power of free markets to regulate sulfur emissions (one of the first "cap-and-trade" programs for a pollutant) was so wildly successful and so widely lauded by both industry and government that most enviros can recite the story in their sleep.[2] Even within businesses, good policy can have huge benefits. BP, for example, created an internal carbon-trading program that simply put a price on emissions—though no money changed hands, the awareness created among the business divisions helped them radically reduce greenhouse gas emissions.

Of course, the government is not faultless, nor is it the only solution. Government can make catastrophically bad decisions that cripple a society for generations. Yet I simply don't see another way out of the climate crisis—or at least, I don't see a path that isn't at least partly illuminated by government policy. I am 100 percent confident that given time and growing energy prices, markets would find a way to solve climate change, as they are already doing in the automobile sector. The problem, as I've said before, is that we don't have the time to wait for that to happen.

Meanwhile, efficiency, for all its truly miraculous promise, just isn't enough. McKinsey and Company estimated that with a return on investment of 10 percent we could cut global energy demand growth in half over fifteen years *without hurting economic growth*.[3] But even in a dream scenario where every opportunity to save energy is seized, global energy use will continue upward, even accelerate. Energy demand from China alone—now two to four times greater than anticipated, according to a new study—would dramatically overshadow the 116 million metric tons of carbon emissions reductions pledged by all the developed countries in the Kyoto Protocol.[4] And even if we achieved Kyoto, we wouldn't be close to solving climate change! To meet its needs, China is now adding a new coal-fired power plant every ten days.[5] Bottom line: We can't get away from adding new supply. At some point, we have to change how we make power—we have to "decarbonize" our power plants.

David and Goliath:
Clean New Power vs. Dirty Old Power

Getting away from carbon-based fuels is tough. At Aspen Skiing Company, we've been working on it for a couple of years now with our utility, Holy Cross Energy. We've gone with Holy Cross to visit potential sites for small hydroelectric plants on the Colorado River, and we've gone down the road quite far with a wind development company doing a mountaintop project nearby. The idea is that these projects would provide power to Holy Cross and thus would get as close as possible to powering our business directly. As with all big projects, there are huge obstacles. When we explored a wind farm high on a ridge in Colorado, the development company had trouble buying turbines, which are in short supply. It wasn't clear if it made sense to do that development on that particular site, or on so small a scale. The hydro project we considered hadn't been permitted by the Federal Energy Regulatory Commission, a process that can take years. Project owners sometimes don't call us back. We've also looked into attaching a hydro turbine to a nearby reservoir. There are pike in the reservoir, however, and these non-native fish can't be allowed out into Colorado streams and rivers. A "fish screen" could cost $1 million and kill the project's return on investment. In the interim, reservoir owners have put a bounty on pike in the hopes that fishermen will catch most of them. Good luck with that.

Of the half-dozen renewable energy projects that Aspen Skiing Company has seriously considered financing, we've pulled off only two, the smallest ones on the table. One of those projects—which at the time was the largest solar array in western Colorado (147 kilowatts, enough to power about 20 homes year-round)—wasn't even initially allowed by county law. We had to ask the county to develop new zoning (they obliged), but it added six months to the timeline.*

You get the picture. Developing any kind of energy production plant is hard, but at least with coal and gas power it's not *new* and hard, and there are big, experienced, powerful interests in charge, all part of a long-established industry that benefits from stable government subsidies, investor support, and well-established contractors that have been building the projects for many decades. As a result, we can't blame our utility for buying into the new Comanche 3 coal plant in southeastern Colorado—they need to provide customers with electricity, and the plant was being built anyway. As we've learned, business as usual is a powerful default setting, and it has the advantage of working pretty well.

Compare the fossil fuel power plant business to the solar industry, which in late 2008 was almost brought to its knees (at least in terms of new projects) by congressional failure to renew production and investment tax credits, a crucial part of the economics of any renewable energy project in the United States. Around the same time, the Bureau of Land Management caused a huge uproar when it declared that ap-

....

*The other project was the Snowmass microhydroelectric plant.

proval of solar development on public lands required "further study." (That suggestion was soon overturned by progressive congresspeople like Colorado's Mark Udall, but it was just another random obstacle the coal folks would never encounter.) Even the successful and growing wind industry is so young that there isn't enough manufacturing capacity to meet demand for the turbines.

Greening Power Supply Is Sexy to Business

Despite the difficulty of building new clean power plants to scale, one substantial ray of light is the growing interest in clean power from the corporate sector.

In the past four years, corporate purchases of renewable energy have become something of an arms race. Big, powerful, influential businesses really, really want this stuff. First, Whole Foods made the biggest buy of renewable energy in corporate history. It was soon surpassed by Vail Resorts, which itself was trumped by Wells Fargo, which was beaten back by previous leaders, like Johnson & Johnson and the Air Force (you heard it right—the U.S. Air Force!). Then Pepsi got in the game and dusted everyone by a mile. But by April 2008, Intel was the number-one purchaser of renewable energy credits (RECs). By the time this book goes to print, no doubt another business will have trumped Intel.

In the case of corporate green power purchases, anytime there's a feeding frenzy, you have to ask: what's so tasty? To answer that, we need to understand just what businesses are buying. And a look into the strange and crazy market for renewable energy credits can help us understand what we might need to do to encourage more real production. Additionally, like turning over a rock, a close look at the REC business reveals an unfortunate truth about our nascent efforts to solve climate change—we're charmed by the quick and easy answers, and not so much by the real and effective (but difficult) solutions.

What Is Green Power?

If you want to buy "green power"—that is, renewably generated electricity that comes from solar, wind, small hydro, biomass, or geothermal sources—you can't plug in directly to, say, a wind farm, because the infrastructure for such a connection doesn't exist. (Nor do the logistics. The wind doesn't blow all the time, so it wouldn't work so well.)

Instead, renewable purchases typically come in the form of renewable energy credits, also known as renewable energy certificates, or RECs. An REC represents the environmental attributes of one megawatt-hour of renewable energy.* Here's a quick explanation of what that means.

Think of the utility grid from which you get your electricity as a reservoir. Both Perrier (carbon-free renewables) and muddy water (dirty fossil–generated power) flow into the reservoir. Even if you're responsible for the Perrier flow-

---

*A megawatt-hour is roughly the amount of electricity it takes to run an average American home for a month.

ing in, you won't get it all out when you dip your cup in for a drink. But the whole reservoir is cleaner for your efforts.

Since people want to buy green power but it's impossible to get a clean drink (meaning, it's impossible to direct specific electrons to a home or business), utilities developed a commodity called an REC. Buy an REC and you can take credit for that clean power. The piece of paper that is an REC says that you "own" that clean electricity in the same way that an investor "owns" the pork bellies he or she bought on the commodities market. As such, RECs are seen as a proxy for buying renewable power directly.*

Some of the revenue from RECs goes to the utility that produced the green power; the rest goes to a middleman. In some cases, RECs thus provide financial support to renewable power generators in the form of a production subsidy. But as we'll learn later, that's not always the case. In some instances, RECs are being bought in arrears: the wind power has already been generated (like buying pork bellies that got eaten last year). In those cases, the REC sales are a boon to the producer, but they didn't make the project happen.

....

*Note that an REC is meant to account for the emissions associated with electricity use only. An "offset," which typically needs to meet much stricter standards, represents a distinct amount of carbon that has been kept out of the atmosphere—like capturing landfill methane or storing carbon dioxide underground. One of the growing concerns about RECs is that they are being used as offsets—which is a bit like using oranges in an apple pie. For example, some groups are selling electricity RECs to offset vehicle miles traveled. The two don't correlate. The complex world of RECs and offsets has been studied in great detail by Dr. Mark Trexler, who is widely regarded as a leader in the art of understanding, explaining, and using offsets. See "Clean Air–Cool Planet" (2006), his group's paper on the offset market.

From the outside, it would appear that businesses "get it." They seem to understand that greening their energy supply is the most fundamental action they can take to address greenhouse gas emissions. A second, and probably driving, reason corporations are buying RECs is that it is a very cheap way to make a major brand positioning statement. Purchasing RECs seems like a very productive use of marketing dollars. Without getting involved in the difficulties of launching new energy projects, a company can say: "We're 100 percent wind-powered." And such a huge statement always garners good press. But it turns out that the reality of these transactions is extremely nuanced, even deceptive. It's not clear that business leaders know what they're buying.

"This is more about choice than it is about cost," the CEO of a nearby Colorado resort said after announcing what was at the time the nation's largest REC purchase in history. "We think it's good business in terms of diversifying the number of fuel sources that we have and reducing our company's dependence on fossil fuels."[6] But as we've seen, an REC doesn't represent a diversified fuel source at all, nor does it reduce a business's dependence on fossil fuels. Actual power still comes from where it always did, and it still fluctuates with the price of fuel.

In buying RECs, most corporations claim that they are either "offsetting" their power purchases or "buying wind energy." Both statements are patently untrue. An REC represents clean electricity, whereas an offset represents a certain amount of actual carbon dioxide kept out of the atmosphere.

A corporation that's buying RECs is no more getting clean power than commodities investors are getting tons of pork bellies delivered to their front porch. One of the rare exceptions to rampant corporate misunderstanding (or, less generously, misrepresentation of REC purchases) is Pepsi. In an AP press release, Pepsi said that it was "following a pledge to purchase enough renewable energy certificates to match the amount of electricity it uses for all of its U.S.-based manufacturing facilities." This is what corporations should be saying, no more, no less.

Yet businesses that buy RECs without understanding them (and that are therefore often making a worthless investment) aren't necessarily deceitful or disingenuous. CEOs purchasing RECs generally feel that this is an important and valuable action. (So did I, for that matter, at one point.) In fact, if you want to buy green power today, RECs are really the most obvious and accessible way to go about it. And businesses should not be expected to be experts on renewable energy. At the same time, due diligence on RECs is critical if you want to protect corporate reputation.

Are RECs Worthless?

It's unarguable that to date corporate reputations have been burnished, if not remade, by large REC purchases, which are lauded by environmental groups, business peers, and government alike. That's why the "100 percent" claim matters so much—it's a real statement, much more so than a lesser percentage.

The elephant standing in the middle of the room when corporate boards decide to buy RECs is that they're not all equal: most of the RECs bought early on by corporations, up to and including Intel's purchase, probably had limited value. It's extremely important to understand what's going on here, because clean energy is *the* crucial piece of solving the climate challenge. Our very future depends on how successfully we separate meaningful action from bogus energy programs.

When Aspen Skiing Company started shopping around, I was offered RECs at close to $1 a megawatt-hour. But at the time the cost of generating that much clean electricity was closer to $45 per megawatt-hour for wind, and a whole lot more for solar. Economics 101 tells us that if something is very cheap, there's a huge supply on the market. Some of those RECs I might have purchased would have been about to expire from a previous calendar year. That is, a wind farm that had been around for several years might not have sold its RECs, which would have been rapidly becoming worthless, because they were about to "expire" and had become too old to meet even basic standards of acceptability. Such a "commodity" isn't just worthless but may also be meaningless. For example, some RECs I was offered would have come from electricity generated at a sawmill, but the sawmill was always up and running—the RECs were just extra money for the mill. Others might have come from a microhydroelectric project that had been around for many years . . . hardly driving progress. To say that either of these REC purchases would have been the equivalent of keeping a certain number of cars off the road each year, the sort of claim businesses often make, would have been absurd.

A slew of news reports have come out in the last couple of years questioning the value of RECs. In "Little Green Lies," an article in the October 19, 2007, issue of *Business Week*, Ben Elgin wrote:

> The trouble stems from the basic economics of RECs. Credits purchased at $2 a megawatt-hour, the price Aspen Skiing and many other corporations pay, logically can't have much effect. Wind developers receive about $51 per megawatt-hour for the electricity they sell to utilities. They get another $20 in federal tax breaks, and the equivalent of up to $20 more in accelerated depreciation of their capital equipment. Even many wind-power developers that stand to profit from RECs concede that producers making $91 a megawatt-hour aren't going to expand production for another $2. "At this price, they're not very meaningful for the developer," says John Calaway, chief development officer for U.S. wind power at Babcock & Brown, an investment bank that funds new wind projects. "It doesn't support building something that wouldn't otherwise be built."*

Randy Udall put the REC problem in stark terms in a scathing online post on December 5, 2006:

----

*Elgin had previously reported on shady RECs for *Business Week*. The article quoted here discussed Aspen Skiing Company's struggles with RECs, among other issues.

Two years ago, we took a stab at building a "zero energy" home here in Colorado. We spent about $35,000 extra on solar photovoltaics and solar hot water and superinsulated walls, and sealed, conditioned crawl spaces and a condensing boiler. We got the utility bill down to about two bucks a day, grid power consumption down to about 1,000 kwh/year. Electric and natural gas emissions fell to about 6,000 pounds a year.

According to REC marketers, we could have bought the same environmental benefit for, say, forty bucks a year. "Ditch the solar, Jenny, I've purchased a century's worth of eco-penance for four grand."[7]

Randy later said of one business that was trying to "green" itself by buying some RECs every month in all of its outlets: "If you can green yourself with fifteen dollars per month, then this ain't the revolution."

Dr. Mark Trexler, managing director of Global Consulting Services at EcoSecurities in Portland, Oregon, is one of the world's leading experts on RECs and offsets. In 2006 he mused: "Although the demand for RECs has . . . been growing, it is quite possible that we are buying and selling large quantities of RECs without materially affecting whether more renewable energy facilities are built. In today's market, the question of whether a new wind farm gets built is usually a function of natural gas prices, falling technology prices, and federal tax incentives, rather than being a function of REC sales."[8]

Meanwhile, many (but not all) of the REC salespeople I talked to had the unmistakable affect of a used-car salesman: "Auden, what's it going to take for me to get you into a soft-top Buick? Here's what I'm going to do for you. . . . " The brokers selling cheap RECs would neither tell me where they came from nor respond in writing to lists of questions. In most conversations, the price of the REC the broker wanted to sell me started high—in the $10 range—and by the end of the conversation it was down in the $2 range. The price of RECs was starting to resemble the price of a rug in Istanbul—totally random, subject to infinite bargaining. What were they really worth? To illustrate the slippery nature of my discussions with REC vendors, I've paraphrased an e-mail exchange I had with a prominent REC vendor regarding the quality of the RECs he was selling.

From: Schendler, Auden [mail to: ASchendler@aspen snowmass.com]

To: REC industry representative

Subject: RECs

REC industry representative:

You are telling me that you are selling $5–8 RECs from wind farms and helping those farms develop, actually MAKING them happen? How is that possible when you're selling RECs for $1–2 each? The price of RECs doesn't scale with the cost of creating a wind farm—a turbine is a million bucks. What are the farms you are working with where this is the case?

Can you answer these questions for me succinctly?

Who are you negotiating with on a new wind farm?

WHERE did you get the RECs you sold to Company X?*

You wouldn't answer this when we talked about RECs initially, and that was one of the reasons we didn't work with you. I don't think I got an answer from you on the phone right now. Where are they coming from?

Are you currently using a forward pricing model?**

In what way do you think the purchase of an REC is improving the global emissions picture? If the answer is that RECs are making the development possible, you've got to show me the math on it. If a turbine costs $1.5 million, how is an REC deal making this happen?

I think the bottom line is that REC brokers are going to have to get a lot more transparent on this to maintain credibility. Buying RECs on discount at the end of the year as they are about to expire, then marking them up and selling them to customers at Company X does not constitute saving the planet. And that's a primary concern for an increasing number of us in the environmental community.

Thanks,

Auden

....

*The specifics of this e-mail have been changed to protect anonymity.

**A forward pricing model means selling RECs before a wind farm is built to finance that wind farm. Because the REC is part of the financial model, the wind farm is being made possible by the REC sales.

From: REC industry representative

To: Schendler, Auden

Subject: RECs

Thanks for the continuing conversation, Auden. I think it might be more fruitful for us to speak in person, as I don't believe a simple e-mail exchange will do justice to the thrust of your questions. Beyond the specific questions you have, I want to say that it's clear to me that you care very deeply about promoting effective environmental solutions. I want you to know that I share that concern. Honestly, I think we each have a lot to learn from each other.

I'll be up in the mountains in early January. Will you be there? Maybe we could meet during or after?

All the best,

REC industry representative

From: Schendler, Auden [mail to:ASchendler@aspen snowmass.com]

To: REC industry representative

Subject: RECs

REC industry representative:

I'm not sure I agree—the problem with the REC industry right now is that these questions can't be answered at all, simply or not. I really need clear yes-or-no or similarly succinct answers here, absent of hypothetical situations. For example, I'm dying to talk to a wind farm developer that can show me how the project was made possible through REC sales. That would answer a ton of questions. Can you connect me with such a person? I won't be at the Vail event, so I'd love it if you could answer my questions below.

Thanks,

Auden

From: REC industry representative

To: Schendler, Auden

Subject: RECs

Auden,

With all due respect, I think answering your questions without discussing the context would be a disservice to the larger goals we share. As you're keenly aware, the REC tool is a complex one. I would appreciate the opportunity to share my insights in a longer conversation before being subjected to uninformed judgments about my intention or my credibility.

Given the opportunity, I'm happy to explain in-depth with you the current economics of wind farms where RECs are making the difference. (Apparently you've seen at least three good examples already in projects others are touting.) We spend a tremendous amount of time educating both our clients and their employees, customers, press, and the communities in which they work about these important environmental benefits.

I hope we will keep an open dialogue going as I think it could be of great service to the industry and present and future consumers.

REC industry representative

I never got an answer to my questions. Compare this evasiveness to the vendor of the RECs we decided to buy, Eric Blank, at Community Energy.

> Auden,
>
> CEI has something like 400–500 MW of REC sales (the majority at prices north of $10/MWh) that has enabled over $600 million worth of wind energy facilities to become economically feasible. . . . It's an incredible success story. . . . This ability to market RECs at these volumes and prices has also drawn major utilities such as Exelon Generation Company, PPL Energy, PECO Energy, and Commonwealth Edison into the wind business as wind power purchasers. . . . There is now a long and clear record that purchases of local wind lead directly to large wind energy investments (and in the case of Pennsylvania four wind turbine generator manufacturing facilities with over 1,000 high-paying jobs).
>
> In regard to the national RECs (priced at $2–3/MWh), I tend to agree that they don't have a tight link to new wind farms (as they're too low-priced to materially influence new development). . . . However, there is still clearly defined value in the REC. . . . The REC is the property right to all environmental and other non-electrical values associated with the wind energy generation (including satisfying RPS [Renewable Portfolio Standards],* carbon credits, NO_x and SO_x** emission

---

*Renewable Portfolio Standards are state requirements that a certain percentage of electricity come from renewable sources of energy.

**NO_x and SO_x are oxides of nitrogen and sulfur, pollutants that cause smog and acid rain. They have been effectively regulated through cap-and-trade programs, the same sorts of programs suggested for regulating carbon dioxide emissions.

allowances going to the wind farm, etc.). . . . Although the future value of a carbon credit associated with wind generation is speculative (carbon regulation is not in place sufficient to provide a clear price, etc.), the underlying property right is real and well defined legally. . . . Also, if anything, RECs are becoming more valuable as CO_2 regulation gets more real and state renewable energy mandates kick in. . . . In fact, you may be able to sell your CEI RECs at a higher price than you paid on the open market as prices have increased over the past six months. . . .

Hope this is responsive. . . . Feel free to call too. . . .

Eric

When we bought RECs, we chose to go with Eric's company for three reasons: First, Community Energy had been vetted for us by a Colorado environmental group specializing in green power; second, we knew that even if our purchase didn't drive new wind production directly, at least our money went to support an organization that was in the business of creating new wind farms; and third, Eric had integrity, as did his business, and he was a known entity in the green power world, with a reputation for getting new wind developed.*

....

*Eric recommended that we buy much higher-quality RECs, but we didn't because it was too expensive and we couldn't get to the 100 percent figure. I talk about this challenge later in this chapter when I suggest that businesses are only interested in cheap RECs. That was certainly the case for us.

Still, I began to wonder: If most businesses are buying the credits from green energy that is being produced anyway, and there's a huge surplus of it on the market, are any of us really driving change? Are there better ways to protect the climate, like directly funding wind farms, or spending that money on lobbying, or developing ways to generate clean power using methane, a highly potent greenhouse gas that is currently vented from coal mines? Are RECs merely the indulgences we buy to escape the twenty-first-century environmental inquisition?

Good vs. Bad RECs

An independent report in 2006 by an NGO called Clean Air–Cool Planet suggested that some consumers are being duped by offsets and RECs for the simple reason that not all RECs are equal. It is important to note that there are both good and bad RECs. The contrast between the two is stark. A bad REC costs about $2 and comes from, say, a wind farm that has been developed already. Bad RECs don't do anything to drive new renewable energy development. Your purchase may be a nice bonus for the wind farm developer, small hydro plant owner, or sawmill (and for the REC broker you bought it from), but it didn't do anything to change carbon dioxide emissions in the atmosphere. You might call this product "vaporware."

Good RECs, on the other hand, actually make new renewable energy development happen. But they tend to be expensive, making it hard for businesses to buy enough to make a big statement and cover all of their electricity use. For example, in 2008 Aspen Skiing Company developed a 147-kilowatt solar energy farm in Carbondale in partnership with the Colorado Rocky Mountain School, a private high school. We sell the project RECs to Xcel Energy at roughly $170 per megawatt-hour over twenty years. (That's what it takes to incentivize new solar development in Colorado!) If you took away these REC sales, our project would collapse because it would have a negative return on investment. So Xcel can rightly claim that its REC purchase created new emissions reduction through green power production.

This sort of REC is called a "forward REC," and in my opinion it is the only kind of REC that matters. Forward RECs tend to be expensive (for wind power they cost $8 and up), and they almost certainly need to be purchased through a long-term contract. (That's because the wind farm developer, for example, needs the commitment to work into its financial models, just as we did with the solar farm.) Two organizations that have long sold these very legitimate forward RECs are Native Energy and Community Energy.

The fundamental concept behind all RECs, proponents argue, is that their sale creates a market mechanism to drive new wind development. Down the road, the theory goes, as more and more people buy RECs, they become more expensive as a result of shrinking supply and increasing demand. As RECs go up in price, they incentivize the development of new renewable power because people want more of those lucrative RECs to sell. To some extent, this is happening. Some REC vendors have told me that "the era of low-priced RECs is over."

There's a looming problem, however. I believe there is corporate demand *only* for cheap RECs, which serve as a remarkable—and remarkably cheap—tool for brand positioning. For only a small fraction of a company's utility bill (1 to 2 percent), it can say it is buying 100 percent clean power.*

But if you jack the price up from $2 to, say, $8 to $10 (roughly the price needed to drive new wind development), suddenly buying RECs is much less of a bargain to the marketing department. What else could you do, from a PR perspective, with that much cash? This is a catch-22: As businesses buy RECs, the price will go up to a point where their value drives new wind development, but when the price reaches that threshold, the large-scale buyers go away.

As all RECs (good and bad) go up in price owing to supply and demand, they will become increasingly important parts of new wind development. But that may be irrelevant. Carbon regulation is soon going to incentivize renewable energy development far more than any REC, while having the added benefit of legitimizing the market through strict standards for what counts as a carbon reduction. When that happens, crappy RECs will go from almost worthless to entirely so, and the whole experience will have been just a game, albeit an informative one.

....

*Even if that claim is disingenuous, as we learned earlier, it's standard practice.

What Good Energy Policy Looks Like

It is important to note that the good government policy I suggest, like carbon regulation—which most lawmakers support—does not involve mandates to "use wind power" or "drive a Prius." Instead, the transformative policies force markets to reflect the true price of power—carbon taxes, for example—thereby sending a signal and letting people and businesses find their own creative solutions.

Occasionally, during presentations, I'm told that subsidies for renewables are bogus and that we should let free markets decide. I ask, "Okay, would you like to eliminate all the subsidies that exist for coal and oil?" And the answer is always, "No," or simply silence. Our markets aren't free, and the role of good regulation is to correct perversions like the price of oil, which has never reflected its true cost in pollution, military presence in the Gulf, or road upkeep. A policy that did reflect oil's true cost would immediately incentivize alternative fuels simply by leveling the playing field, not by offering heavy-handed subsidies.

Developing good policy in the United States is also crucial because other nations will follow. A standard climate delayer tactic is to ask, "Why do anything if China and India won't act?" But who are we kidding? Those countries won't do a thing until the United States does something, because we have always been the world's leading consumers of energy; we also followed a similar route to economic development that used cheap and dirty power. We got ours, and they will feel they deserve theirs. But if we start deploying renewable technologies, their response might well be: "What do they know that we don't?" Global policy change has to start in the United States.

Concrete and Steel Solutions

In the absence of any policy leadership, the REC debacle was inevitable, as well as symptomatic of our times. Churchill said that Americans could be counted on to do the right thing . . . after they had exhausted all other alternatives. RECs and our focus on corporate green reputation seem to illustrate this. We are exhausting all other alternatives before finally getting down to the business of climate protection.

As Randy Udall wrote in a Web post:

> Touting your carbon neutrality is a sign that you don't get it. Climate change isn't about you, it's not about marketing, it's not a friggin' bragfest, particularly when you don't have much to brag on. In a way, and this is the ultimate heresy, it's not even about reducing your emissions. Whole Foods won't be carbon neutral until Wal-Mart and the rest of the nation's big boxes are; that is, it won't be carbon neutral until we have radically transformed the entire energy infrastructure on which we depend. This is the work of the next few decades, maybe the next few generations. It's not a marketing stratagem, a contest, a parlor game, a cheap trick.

The good news is that the renewable energy sector—
overwhelmingly without REC sales as an incentive—is
growing wildly. China is a great example. Despite its huge
and growing reliance on dirty coal power, it is also the
world's leading producer of renewable energy and is on the
way to overtaking developed countries in creating clean technologies, according to a report by the nonprofit Climate
Group.[9] But while this is encouraging—the market is picking up on the value of clean energy—it's not happening at
remotely close to the scale necessary to solve climate change.
That will require national policy.

According to the recent UN Environment Program report *Global Trends in Sustainable Energy Investment 2008*, financial markets invested a record $148.4 billion in the
renewable energy and energy efficiency sectors in 2007, a 60
percent increase over the previous year.* (The U.S. government, by comparison, annually throws a few billion dollars
toward renewables and efficiency R&D—about what Americans spend on Halloween each year.)

Moving forward, the lesson to take from the REC debacle is the same lesson we've learned elsewhere in this book:
we have to be clear-eyed and realistic about what matters and
what doesn't. Aspen Skiing Company has taken its search for
clean energy in a new direction: In one case, we're entering
into a power purchase agreement with a utility that is developing a wind farm. If we agree to buy power over twenty
years at a fixed premium, the utility will install four new tur-

---

*United Nations Environment Program, 2008.

bines and we will get the power from those units. Like a forward REC, this agreement makes a new project happen, putting steel in the ground. At the same time, we're exploring small hydroelectric plants on our four mountains to provide some of our power, which we will sell locally if we have a surplus. We've got one small plant already up and running at Snowmass, making $15,000 worth of clean energy each year. This solution, which uses existing snowmaking infrastructure, taps historical precedent: until 1957, all of Aspen ran on such small hydro systems; some are still running, and others are being recommissioned.

Think about that: not too long ago—in only 1957—a place like Aspen had already substantially cracked the sustainability nut by solving the power supply puzzle. It was done with ingenuity, but also with hard labor, concrete, and iron, creating a tangible solution no one could doubt the value of.

It seems reasonable, and not overly optimistic, to think we can do it again.

Green Buildings:
Simple, Elegant, and Crucial

And the shadows filling up this land
Are the ones I built with my own hand.

—EMMYLOU HARRIS, "PRAYER IN OPEN D"

An architect in Santa Fe named Ed Mazria has convincingly argued that buildings—or more broadly, architecture—are responsible for almost half of global greenhouse gas emissions and that, as such, they are the key to solving the climate challenge.

There are more than 130 million buildings in the United States. Almost all of them are on life support, like patients in intensive care. Moreover, the impacts of assembling, heating, cooling, and electrifying buildings are rising rapidly. Buildings consume one-quarter of the global wood harvest, one-sixth of its fresh water, and two-fifths of material and energy flows. In the United States, buildings account for 65 percent of electricity consumption and 36 percent of primary energy use; operating a typical American house produces 26,000 pounds of greenhouse gases each year, enough to fill the

Goodyear blimp.[1] Mazria notes that buildings are "the most long-lived physical artifacts society produces." So buildings, new and existing, are really the linchpin in solving the climate crisis.[2]

There is a strong case to be made that there is already a booming green building movement. Membership in the U.S. Green Building Council (USGBC), a green building trade group, is growing exponentially, from 250 members to 6,000 in a few years; recently membership has reached upward of 17,000. States and big municipalities like Seattle and Portland, Salt Lake City and Denver, are adopting the LEED (Leadership in Energy and Environmental Design) certification system for public buildings. Numerous federal programs have evolved to support green building. There is reasonably strong federal leadership on the issue, and corporate leadership is expanding.

In fact, in the last decade something exciting has happened in the green building world. Conferences on the topic, which used to be love-ins featuring hippies in beads and Birkenstocks, are moving into the mainstream, thus encouraging business participation. In the past decade, the USGBC has given the field a professional sheen and helped it blossom. The USGBC attracted over twenty thousand people to its Chicago conference in 2007. Bill Clinton spoke. Many attendees were wearing suits, and the whiff of serious money was in the air. At a previous conference, the head of China's construction administration—which will be responsible for much of the construction the world will see in the coming decade—got a standing ovation. There were also product suppliers, architects, consultants, builders, engineers, academics, doctors, and scientists. The conferences have become a runaway train of enthusiasm for green buildings.

But despite the new popularity of building green and all its benefits—better buildings, healthier, happier, more productive workers, energy savings, aesthetics—green building has been agonizingly slow to take off.

Why Is Green Building So Hard?

Not long ago, an article in *Colorado Company* magazine highlighted the partners in Dorado Developments, a company that differentiates its business in one way: It believes in nothing but green building. This was a wonderful story. But it brings up a question: Why was this still a story at all? Despite all the buzz surrounding green building, the mass-market building sector remains oblivious to the issue. Most of the structures in building magazines like *Architectural Record* and *Architectural Digest* are not green.

It's easy to get so completely immersed in the sustainability business that you think it's happening everywhere. The illusion is that a revolution is afoot. Unfortunately, that appears to be true only as long as it takes you to look around. Try to buy a green home in any major subdivision in America. Good luck. In both the commercial and residential sectors, green building remains the exception, like a flower in the desert. And while more and more major developers are pursuing a nominal green agenda, it's still hard to get at the real energy reductions needed when their projects

come to fruition. Meanwhile, even good green builders—
the best— often put in a suboptimal performance or fail entirely. Renowned green architect William McDonough's
Environmental Studies Center at Oberlin College is a relevant case study. That project became legendary for its in-
ability to meet the hype of its designer. Even at Aspen
Skiing Company, where we *get it* and have pulled off exceptional green buildings, we struggle. On one recent project,
communications snafus led to the energy efficiency in a project being substantially cut, and it felt like I was battling the
engineer and architect who were working for us, a dis-
turbingly familiar feeling.

In the environmental building community here in Colorado, everyone's got a story of a disastrous effort: one that
used ten times as much energy as it was supposed to; a mi-
croturbine that turned out to be not so cost-effective, even
after it was reinstalled correctly, because gas prices spiked; a
south-facing community college that needed air conditioning retrofitted in the winter.

Wait! Green building was supposed to be the road to the
promised land, the place where good design meshes with environmental stewardship for the benefit of all and leaves the
bottom line intact. Instead, if Moses had been an architect,
he would have come back from the mountain with ten
tablets of screw-ups, cover-ups, and new ways to meet code
in the most expensive ways possible. In short, the question
that should be dogging the construction industry is this:
Why is green building so hard?[3]

Time Is Running Out

One answer is that change takes time. The problem—one of my mantras in this book—is that we don't have time. To stabilize atmospheric carbon dioxide concentrations at twice preindustrial levels, we have to displace seven gigatons of CO_2 a year. Buildings are a big part of that equation, and we have to cut those gigatons soon. In fact, we have to cut them *now* if we want to reduce emissions radically in the next decade. That's why the slow growth of the movement is alarming.

We must look for ways to speed up the adoption of green practices and ways to break down the barriers to a pervasively green construction industry. Some of the reasons for the slow adoption are obvious and well studied: up-front costs; the problems and cultural resistance associated with any new and different approach; lack of talent or expertise; lack of research, funding, and awareness; perceived trade-offs between quality or security and sustainability; decades of ingrained practice with inefficient construction; bad building codes; and finally, people's unwillingness to admit mistakes.

One of the main reasons green building hasn't become mainstream faster is that the practice is often presented as a secret language, a form of Esperanto spoken only by William Shatner and a few weirdos in the Haight-Ashbury. Tell me you haven't heard the term "Green Mafia." It means *that* guy knows the secret handshake. And by definition, you don't.

I am repeatedly confronted with individuals, builders, even architects who clearly perceive green building as complex, even unknowable. It isn't. (Though it's not easy. But as a friend has said: "*Nothing* in business is easy. Should we be surprised?") Nonetheless, it seems like nobody's making an effort to discourage the perception that green building theory is a foreign language.

The USGBC and LEED

The good news is that the idea—if not the practice—of green building has become understandable, even sexy, to the masses. For this, we have to thank Leadership in Energy and Environmental Design, or LEED, the flagship program of the U.S. Green Building Council. LEED is a certification program designed to rate a building's environmental performance. It provides a means for novices to create, understand, and certify buildings. It created a national standard for green buildings where none existed before. The leading effort to bring green building to the mainstream, LEED has done wonderful things for the movement since its inception in 2000. It is the number-one reason green building hasn't festered in a small, dark, and radical corner of the construction world.

Prior to LEED, "green building" was all in the eye of the claimant: you could, for example, ban smoking and call your restaurant green. Why not? There was no standard, so any claim was as plausible as the next. LEED changed that, tapping a pent-up demand for reliable information with a rig-orous rating system and a checklist for going green.

In launching LEED, the USGBC created a buzz around green building and formalized, standardized, even Oprah-ized the field—just what was needed. It enlisted the eager partici-pation of many thousands of building professionals. The USGBC deserves endless credit for wrestling with the com-plex question of what makes a building green and expanding the answer beyond energy to encompass water efficiency, site issues, resource efficiency, and indoor environmental quality. Recognizing that the conventional approach to construc-tion is brain-dead, more than sixty thousand design profes-sionals have trained to become "LEED accredited." Overnight, LEED became a dominant global brand, like Nike in athletic shoes or Dell in personal computers. Now, if you don't have "LEED Accredited Professional" on your business card, you're just not *all that* anymore. Equally im-portant, LEED has helped reduce the troubling plague of greenwashing.

When LEED was launched, it provoked so much enthu-siasm that it became synonymous with "green." The message was, you have to know LEED if you want to build green. The problem is that, not only is this not true, but LEED it-self is sometimes an obstacle to getting green done. LEED is necessary, but it is also imperfect and complicated.

Because you can't talk about green building without talk-ing about LEED, and because I've been involved with the program since its inception, I'll give you some history here.

LEED: A Tool and an Obstacle

By 2005, if not earlier, LEED had become the last word on green building, and it is even more powerful today. That makes it even more imperative that the program work very, very well. For all the program's good qualities and all the improvements to it since its inception, there remain three outstanding challenges facing LEED today. Some of these problems would be endemic to any certification program, but they are worth discussing because green building is so important to the future of the planet that we absolutely must get it right.

First, it's damn hard (costly, complicated, and tedious) to get certified, so not that many buildings have achieved the goal. Second, LEED doesn't emphasize energy enough (though it is rapidly improving on that point). And third, LEED is fundamentally a certification system but gets treated as a guide to green building.

The Few and the Proud

Despite the fact that LEED is extremely popular, surprisingly few buildings have been certified. To be certified to LEED standards, designers use a checklist to determine their success in reducing impacts in five categories: site planning, energy consumption, water usage, indoor environmental quality, and building materials. Pay a modest fee, satisfy the prerequisites, acquire twenty-six of sixty-nine possible points, and your building can become "LEED-certified."

Once a building is completed, a developer submits documentation to the USGBC, where a third-party evaluator determines whether to award a certified Silver, Gold, or Platinum rating. It is very difficult to grab the Platinum ring: Worldwide there are only fifty-three such buildings in the commercial sector. Indeed, it's hard to get a building certified at all. The program began in 2000, and there are 1,753 certified projects (in the new commercial division) over seven years; 14,390 were registered but not certified as of September 2008. With more than 130 million buildings in the United States alone, that number seems small.

Randy Udall and I wrote a paper in 2005 that pointed out that this number was not transformative. Our criticism, based on personal experience certifying buildings, including one of the first eleven LEED structures in the world, was that the program had become costly, clumsy, difficult to implement, and enormously bureaucratic. We found that many builders were saying, "No thanks," because the costs of certification were too high, or they were more interested in using the additional money for green measures like solar panels. We cannot afford for this to happen; we need as many flagship buildings as possible to help spread the green building message.

The USGBC has made a good-faith effort to address these concerns, and the process has become easier over the years. In its defense, LEED doesn't aspire to be a system that captures the bulk of the market; instead, it's meant as a stamp of approval for only the very best buildings.*

Proponents rightfully argue that LEED was always meant to be a guiding light, not a code for the world. Leadership programs and certification always start small. Only a few people win gold medals at the Olympics, but those winners can drive a generation of change, as Lance Armstrong did when he popularized road biking in America. We don't all need to be like Lance, but one Lance can help change the world.

But the very exclusivity of a LEED ranking is why flaw number two—the fact that you can certify a building to a high LEED standard without all that much in the way of energy efficiency—is so serious. If only a few buildings are going to get the LEED imprimatur, then it should really mean something special, like the Medal of Honor.

Energy Is All

Willa Cather once said: "The road is all."** She meant, in the Zen sense, that it's the journey, not the destination, that matters in life. In green building, you might say, "Energy is all."

....

*That said, why not start to bulk-certify buildings using a process like IRS tax audits? Speaking as a corporate executive, I can tell you that if we built ten LEED buildings and the USGBC decided to audit only two of them, we'd build each to the same standard. Skimping—and the risk that we'd get caught—would be a devastating credibility hit to our business and a risk we certainly wouldn't take— nor would other businesses.

**"The end is nothing, the road is all," is the famous Cather quote. It was probably the French historian Jules Michelet—whom Cather was fond of quoting— who first said this.

Unfortunately, until recently, many LEED buildings had not achieved anything beyond business as usual on the energy front—the only front that really matters. There was concern about this as early as 2004, when Jay Stein and Rachel Buckley at E Source argued that achieving LEED doesn't necessarily mean anything in that the certified buildings might or might not be better than ordinary structures.[4]

The reason I know about LEED buildings that don't do much with energy is that Aspen Skiing Company built one. The Sundeck Restaurant on Aspen Mountain was one of the first ten LEED structures in the United States, one of only eleven in the world. As participants in LEED 1.0, our experiences helped develop LEED 2.0. But with the Sundeck, we got into the process late and as a result weren't able to redesign the building envelope and HVAC system for maximal efficiency. Because we could pick points from a range of areas and didn't have to do anything exceptional on energy, we got certified anyway. The certification gave us enormous credibility and got us huge amounts of press. (And we deserved it for a variety of non-energy-related work we did, including fully deconstructing, salvaging, grinding, and composting the previous structure, a project that became a model for the region.) But you have to ask the question: If climate change is the issue of our time, and if the most significant way to address it is through building efficiency, how can a building be called green if few to no energy efficiency measures are incorporated into it?

Joe Lstiburek is a ridiculously credentialed (he's got a bachelor of science degree, a master's in engineering, a PhD, and an engineering license), wickedly bright, eagerly combative, and hilariously funny forensic engineer who investigates building failures. As an internationally recognized authority on building design, he has said: "Build your building. Look at the utility bills. Compare them to an older building. If they are not lower, then shut the fuck up." He's got a point.

The issue ultimately becomes one of greenwashing. On October 19, 2005, the *Wall Street Journal* ran a story on the cover of its "Marketplace" section about 30 Hudson Place, the Goldman Sachs skyscraper, a building that achieved LEED certification at the lowest level.[5] The building achieved exactly zero credits for energy efficiency or renewable energy. Not a single one. Despite the fanfare of the certification and its prominent placement in the *Wall Street Journal*, 30 Hudson Place simply isn't a green building.

And yet, ironically, LEED was created, to some extent, to prevent greenwashing! Post-LEED, in theory, no one can take minor measures like installing recycled bathroom dividers and declare a building green. That's why it's so important that LEED certification should mean something. The USGBC agrees and in 2007 increased the baseline requirement for energy efficiency so that any new commercial LEED structure must beat an aggressive energy code by 14 percent; further energy requirements are apparently in the works. This is a good start, and even that 14 percent is fairly stringent, going above and beyond an already strict code; it's also challenging to achieve because LEED takes into account "process loads" like dishwashers or computers. But read only a little bit of Ed Mazria—or the latest climate science reports—and you'll realize it's not enough. (That's why Mazria started his own program, called Architecture 2030, to push for even more aggressive targets and eventually carbon neutrality.)

One of the reasons buildings sometimes score high on the LEED chart but low on the energy scale is that the program is a *certification*, not a construction guide.

It's a Test, Not a Guide

When I was a student at Stuyvesant High School in New York, we studied to the tests, and we were damn good at it. If you did anything less than 95 on the state Regents exams each year, people worried that you might have cognitive problems or wax in your ears. But while I got really good at taking tests—a skill that served me very well—I didn't learn all that much in high school other than how to take tests. The same problem has evolved with LEED: builders are designing to LEED points instead of designing green buildings.

This inevitable result, which isn't the USGBC's fault, is what I call "point-mongering." Instead of creating a building that is comprehensively green, designers and builders start by seeing how many, and which, credits they can get at the lowest cost. For example, if you get one point for improving the efficiency of the heating system, at great expense, and one point for installing a bike rack and an on-site shower for commuters, you're likely to go for the latter, even though the former has vastly greater environmental benefits. The way around this might be for the USGBC to develop a green design protocol, something I take a stab at later in this chapter. And another way around it, already in use to some extent, is to make certain that vital credits, like energy efficiency, are prerequisites for certification.

A colleague of mine just went to a one-day seminar on green building that was billed as a primer on the subject. I had hoped it would be a soup-to-nuts discussion of how to build environmentally responsible structures. What are some examples of how it works and doesn't? What do we have to do to make it successful? What does a good wall look like in a commercial building? But the seminar was not what I had hoped—it was an eight-hour discussion of LEED.

The tendency to study to the test with LEED is endemic, and at Aspen Skiing Company we're as guilty as anyone. On a recent project, the lead engineer told the project manager that it would be too expensive to meet "LEED Gold" standards on energy, and as a result, many of the progressive efficiency measures were cut. Admittedly, we were on a tight time frame and over budget already. But the discussion masked a fundamental misunderstanding: LEED Gold is not an energy standard. It's just a rating. In fact, the building in question looks like it will do very, very well on LEED, perhaps achieving Gold. But if in the process we miss the one thing that matters—energy efficiency—that Gold rating will feel hollow.*

....

*Horrifyingly, this means I am now in the process of LEED-certifying another ASC building with minimal energy efficiency measures, something I swore I'd never do. To explain how this happened in a business that "gets it" would require several hours at the bar. The fault was mine, and the barriers were communication, money, and human factors. But the fact of my failure only underlines the extreme difficulty with successful green construction and the truly staggering nature of the challenge of solving climate change.

In the end, we need LEED. We need the excitement it brings, the understanding it provides, the momentum it has developed, and the movement it has spawned. Like any large and complicated program, it has its problems, but it would be impossible to create a certification that is trouble-free or one that wouldn't be gamed by some participants. LEED has inspired a generation, and as it grows and improves it will inspire many more. Meanwhile, the people running LEED are smart and eager to improve the program. The organization's president, Rick Fedrezzi, is open-minded, open to criticism, and change-oriented in a way that is rare for humans, let alone leaders of large bureaucracies. He seems to recognize Ben Franklin's maxim that "our critics are our friends because they show us our faults." I endorse LEED, use it myself, recommend it to others, and only offer criticism to improve it.

So, use LEED. Enjoy it. Get kudos for certification. And don't forget the energy efficiency.

Scrapping Biomimicry for Simplicity

LEED isn't the only thing that contributes to the notion that green building is some sort of secret language. One annoying school of obfuscation that has evolved in the green building community is called "biomimicry," the idea that buildings should be modeled on natural systems. Nature has done millions of years of research, the argument goes, so why not tap into that? If we could only learn how spiders make thread stronger than steel at room temperature, or how clams make

ceramic at ocean temperatures, we'd be on our way to crack-
ing some major energy challenges and building obstacles.

But here's the problem: buildings aren't clams or spiders.
For starters, they don't move around or eat bugs. As Dr.
Mike Brown, an environmental consultant and editor at the
Journal of Industrial Ecology points out, biomimicry seems to
be about making goals that are simple and straightforward—
avoid toxics, strive for closed loops, minimize energy, and so
on—into something that requires a consultant to explain
how you should imitate nature. As a result, it takes green
building away from the masses and keeps it in the ivory
tower. But green building is not ivory tower stuff, even if it's
hard to actually pull off. In most cases what you need is
pretty basic: passive solar orientation and thermal mass, if
possible; envelope efficiency, including superinsulation and
tightness; and an efficient and right-sized heating system.
You don't need a consultant, a biologist, or a PhD.

The problem with biomimicry, LEED as design guidance
instead of certification, and other fads is that they fog the
glass: we know what it takes to make an efficient building.
Here in Aspen we're building new affordable housing of mod-
ular construction that uses thick insulation, krypton gas–filled
windows, and an efficient heating system. Boom—done.
We're going to *crush* the energy code with these buildings—
and stay on budget. As project manager Mark Vogele told
me: "See, Auden, it's not all that damn complicated!" And
that's true: once you get it, as Mark does, it's relatively easy.
It's just that to most contractors it's all new.

Forgive Me, Father, I Don't Have the Money

As with everything in the sustainability business, the hurdles in the building process aren't technological. So what are they? Often, it comes down to money.

Here's a case study that illustrates the tensions that can arise between green champions and contractors: The building is either in the design phase or designed and ready to go. The green champion says: "Look, I know your budget is fixed. But for just 10 percent more, spent now, for some better heating and cooling equipment, window upgrades, and some other minor efficiency tweaks, you could construct a building that would use half (or one-third of, or 20 percent of . . .) the energy over the fifty- to one-hundred-year (or longer) life cycle of the building. And the return on investment for that is under ten years!" Between the lines of such talk the message typically is: "Don't you understand what I'm telling you? It's so frickin' *obvious*! Why don't you simpletons use life-cycle analysis?"*

But the contractor says: "I understand the benefits. I beg your pardon, but I'm not stupid. I understand life-cycle analysis. But my budget is fixed. I don't have any more money. I can't get any more. What do you want me to do? *I just don't have the money.*"

....

*Life-cycle analysis is a technique that takes into account the costs associated with a building or product over its whole life, not just in the production or construction phase. If you do the life-cycle analysis on a new car purchase, for example, you might decide to get something with better gas mileage.

Green designers rightfully point out that the decisions you make and the money you spend in the first tiny fraction of a building's life influence that building forever. But if you don't have the money, you don't have the money.

There is a way around this challenge of up-front costs, and leave it to Harvard to have found a solution. Tom Vautin, Harvard's associate vice president for facilities and environmental services, realized that the university wasn't installing the best equipment with long-term energy savings owing to up-front costs. And he recognized that the issue was purely economic: buildings with long lives should have the best, most energy-efficient equipment. What Vautin did, for purely financial reasons, was set up a revolving loan fund. Project managers who wanted, say, an extra $50,000 for a 96 percent efficient boiler instead of an 86 percent efficient boiler could dip into the fund during building construction and pay the money back out of the energy savings compared to the energy budget for the less efficient boiler. The fund is at work at Harvard today. It ensures that the buildings are the best they can be, and it has the added benefit of protecting the climate every time it gets used. (In the real world, where I dwell, even an elegant program like Tom's can hit a wall. The most prominent barrier in many companies is management's refusal to recognize the savings—for example, your budget gets lowered to the new energy-efficient standard. This happens all the time with "performance contracting," where firms do efficiency retrofits for free and plan to get paid out of savings. Clients sometimes dispute the existence of the savings. Just like at the Nell. D'oh!)

Another up-front cost reality manifests itself through a process called "value engineering," a term that is just about the sum of all problems in building design. Value engineering (which, Amory Lovins points out, doesn't add value and isn't engineering) is a cost-cutting exercise conducted just before the building's design gets final approval. It typically involves eliminating things or downgrading materials or systems with reference only to first costs, never to longer-term benefits.

At a building project at Aspen Highlands, we value-engineered out some windows in a building because we couldn't afford them. When our staff occupied the building, it was so hot and stuffy that they couldn't function. So the next year we retrofitted the windows into the blank walls at about three times the cost of the initial installation.

It cost a lot more to put the windows in after the fact, but if you wanted windows, *that was the only way it could happen*! Ironically, if we could go back and do it again, we'd have no choice but to do exactly what we did . . . *because we didn't have the money*! (Though, to be fair, we've changed since then. If I presented the case to our CFO Matt Jones today, he'd find the money.)

The reality here is that the idea that it shouldn't—or doesn't—cost more to build green is hogwash. Green construction is still relatively new. As a result, it is a departure from business as usual. The second you depart from standard practice, you are spending time figuring out the new process—with meetings, consultants, and product suppliers. With the first meeting on greening (and there is never just one), you are already adding cost to a project. Plus, by building green, you're building something better. That costs more, too. Always. But it's worth it, and eventually we'll figure it out.

Net-Zero-Energy Monster Homes?

In Aspen, the most iconic symbol of consumption is the trophy home—the city has 150 monster mansions with floor areas greater that 10,000 square feet. In the summer of 2008, the *Denver Post* reported on Aspen's vacation homes as energy hogs. Citing "the whirring motors of cigar humidors and wine cellars, and the flicking on and off of 24/7 floodlights," the report summarized a study by the Sopris Foundation, an Aspen nonprofit, which found that, "with their heated driveways, outdoor hot tubs and 24-hour surveillance systems, Aspen's vacation homes each use more electricity than a block of average American homes. . . . As a result, the luxurious second homes generate most of the town's residential greenhouse gases, even though many of them are occupied only a few weeks each year."[6] They emit more carbon than Aspen's fully occupied homes, according to the study. The *Post* concluded that, "while disproportionate energy use in second homes exists in every mountain-resort community, it is most pronounced in Aspen, where conspicuous consumption is a status symbol."

Anson Fogel of In Power Systems in Carbondale, not far from Aspen, has built a business around cutting energy use in trophy homes. He's an entrepreneur who "can't help but start businesses." A tech-head with red hair, a twinkle in his eyes, and a booming bass voice that seems like it might be coming from somewhere else in the room, Anson is a slight man with the build of an endurance athlete—which he is. He's a backcountry skiing fanatic. He would be just the right guy for the property management firm that called me to ask about greening its business.

Anson has a formula for cutting energy use in trophy homes. For new homes, he says, you do absolutely everything you can to build envelope efficiency (good insulation in walls and roof, good windows, and airtightness). Then you heat and cool the building by using a "geoexchange" system: tapping the relative warmth of the ground in winter and its relative coolness in summer. These systems are also called ground source heat pumps. You make sure lighting, appliances, and controls are state-of-the-art. You use solar thermal to get the high-temperature water you need, and then you add as much solar electric as you need to make up the difference. The result: a net-zero-energy home. Anson himself lives in one.

Of course, though Anson made his own home a net-zero-energy one, convincing others to do this is a different story. Early on in the design phase of one project (the perfect time to start), he met with the architect (from an elite firm of course), the mechanical engineer, the landscape architect, and the owner of a planned twenty-thousand-square-foot second home in Aspen.

Anson talked about the continuum of opportunity— would the owner like to address 5 percent of the structure's energy use? Or 10 percent? Or 100 percent?

The owner said, unequivocally, "I just want to do this 100 percent. It's the right thing to do. I want to go for it."

The first step in the process is figuring out how much energy a building will use, because that determines how much expensive solar energy you need to install after you've mitigated everything as far as possible. So Anson called the engineer. "Have you done any energy modeling on this using Energy 10 software?"

"What's Energy 10? No, modeling is not in the budget. We don't even know how to model it."

So Anson went to the architect to find money to get the model done. The architect talked to the owner, and they said: "This is all too complicated. Can't we just have the payback info on the systems? We already paid the engineer $25,000 so far; we don't have the money in the budget. Can you do a back-of-the-napkin analysis for us?"

Against his better judgment, and at a cost of about $1,000 (pro bono), Anson did the analysis and showed that simply using the best boilers and state-of-the-art controls, the building would have a thirty-year energy cost of $10 million, which presumed increases in energy costs.

To address this kind of energy use, Anson offered three options. The state-of-the-art systems approach, with good building envelope, boilers, and controls, would be good. It would be even better, he said, to install a geoexchange system, which would only add about $300,000 to the cost of the project (out of a total cost of, conservatively, $10 million). This would cut energy use in half. The best approach would be then to install 175 kilowatts of solar on the site to mitigate the remaining energy use.

The engineer said: "Geoexchange won't work."

The owner, no longer excited about the zero energy thing, said: "Okay, we'll delete the pool."

The design team said: "There's no room for all those solar panels, and besides, nobody wants to see them."

So Anson met with the landscape architects to see where they could put the solar panels by getting creative—using not just the roof but the yard, features in the yard, birdbaths, the whole gamut. They found enough area to locate seventy-five kilowatts—not nearly what they needed, but a good effort nonetheless. When the architect met with the approving body in the county to review the plans, the solar wasn't even on the docket. But somehow the topic came up, and the review agents said, in effect, "Good luck. We're never going to let you put any of that up. Anyway, there are going to be better, easier, more efficient ways to do that in the future that aren't so visible. You should wait for that technology."

Anson went back and met with the team. "How do we get this done?" he asked. They said, almost in a chorus, "Never mind. It's too complicated. The owner has decided to back-burner energy efficiency and renewables. Let's can the whole thing." And they did.

In the postmortem, Anson points out three barriers that are hard to overcome. The first is that the media (aided by the Bush administration) perpetuate the myth that technology is evolving and if we just wait something will get developed to solve our problems cheaper, smaller, and easier (Joe

Romm's "technology trap"). As a result, people can justify inaction. (Exhibit A was the Bush administration's focus on hydrogen as a transportation fuel, a technology that is twenty years out from mainstream use, if it happens at all.) As Anson points out, the technology *has* evolved, and the price has come down . . . and in the end the sun hitting the earth's surface only provides about one hundred watts of energy per square foot, so no matter how efficient solar panels get (and they are now between 14 and 18 percent efficient at converting sunlight to electricity), they're still going to need some space.

The second barrier is that the approvals process often makes new or creative projects like Anson's impossible. County approval boards never want to support anything perceived as ugly; in addition, they are often overwhelmed with work and don't have time to answer questions that are new and different (curveballs like "can you dig geoexchange wells outside the property line?").*

In the end, as Anson glumly concludes, "The reality is nobody really wants to do anything." His point: Business as usual rules. This is somewhat of an overstatement, since Anson makes his living in part by working with people who do want to do things and are pretty excited about it. But the challenges of moving the mainstream remain.

The third barrier is the ultimate problem of cost, which can never be too low for people. Cost will always be a barrier.

....

*Or in our experience with the CRMS solar project described in Chapter 7: "Can we legally build a solar farm on agricultural land?"

Anson describes a dreadlocks-wearing hippie biking up to him at a coffee shop on an $8,000 mountain bike and asking what it would take to make her house net-zero-energy. The answer was $35,000, of which $20,000 would come back in rebates. "Holy cow, that is way too expensive!" (*No, it's almost free,* Anson thought.) "They need to bring the price down." But "they" *have* brought the price down. And for the price of the bicycle, the hippie could have been halfway there.

A Silver Lining?

Even though Anson failed with some trophy homes (but not all—he's got many successful projects completed or in progress), something interesting has happened to his business. It's not the very rich but the middle class, living "downvalley" from Aspen, who have taken on the idea of net-zero-energy and are implementing it, often investing what is a huge amount of cash relative to their net worth. And business is booming. Why is this happening with the middle class much more so than with the wealthy?

Anson answers: "Because it's easier on all levels: regulatory, aesthetic, engineering effort (smaller projects), neighborhood amenability—and the homeowners are less busy. They are more likely to think it will make them look smarter/cooler/more responsible." And maybe that's because they actually live in the houses they're trying to fix. Finally, a high energy bill for a middle-class homeowner is more than just a blip on the monthly budget.

Meanwhile, second homes are widely seen as a massive drain on the community. They are empty most of the year, exacerbating an already desperate housing problem since they take up space where some local might be living (although the average price of a home in Aspen is $5 million, so few working-class people can afford to live there). The big homes use energy even when empty. And they create jobs without doing anything to house the workers. In fact, just by existing, these homes make housing even harder to come by.

But there's an opportunity to be had through net-zero-energy trophy homes in Aspen. If you have a house that uses no energy, by definition it's a house with solar panels that generate power. When a house with solar panels is standing empty, it's not entirely useless: it can feed clean power into the local utility grid, becoming a source of green energy for the city, what's called a "distributed power plant."

Adam Palmer: Another View from the Trenches

To understand the challenges facing green building so that we can do it better, we need to get even more granular than Anson's perspective. We need to know what the contractor is saying on the ground, day to day, on a green project. Adam Palmer is the guy to talk to about that. He runs the green building program of Eagle County, Colorado, and he's a true believer. He built his own house in super-green fashion, living the vision. In his midthirties, Adam was Vail Resorts' environmental coordinator for a number of years, and during that time he cycled across the United States as part of a team in the "Race Across America." Adam is a joker, often delivering dry wisecracks so casually you don't see them coming. And he's got a mischievous glint in his eyes that makes him well suited to the battles he fights on building design. He doesn't take himself too seriously.

Adam has his own litany of the obstacles that builders face in the real world. I quote him here at length because he's the consummate green building geek and a true trench warrior.

"First, let's say John Green wants to build a green home and has done his research, bought the land, gets a good artichoke* and enginerd** who designs a great solar-oriented, well-insulated home and got the big stuff right. Then he goes to hire a general contractor. These guys are the bulldogs, in the trenches, and experts in their field with years of experience. Most tell me they think green building is great and they'll do whatever the owner wants, but when it comes down to it, my experience has been that they'll talk you out of just about everything you want to do outside conventional construction. Oh yeah, and enginerds and architightwads† are the butts of all their jokes.

....

*Greenspeak slang for architect.

**Slang for engineer, meaning a mechanical engineer who designs heating and cooling systems.

†Architects.

MR. GREEN: We want to use ICFs for the foundation.*

MR. CONTRACTOR: Those things are crap, can't get 'em straight, you'll blow 'em out, better not do it. You don't need to insulate your foundation here, it's the banana belt.

MR. GREEN: We want to do a shallow frost-protected foundation with fly-ash concrete.

MR. CONTRACTOR: Huh? (*spits*)

MR. GREEN: We want to use SIP panels for the exterior walls.**

MR. CONTRACTOR: Those are too expensive, takes too long to order, what if there's a mistake, the electrician won't like it, stud framing is good enough, and anything beyond R-19 insulation won't pay for itself.

MR. GREEN: We want a solar hot water system.

MR. CONTRACTOR: I know a guy who put one in that totally broke after a few years and didn't work worth a shit. It would be a complete waste of money, and you'd be an idiot. Spend that money on donations to the Sierra Club.

MR. GREEN: We want a radon mitigation system.

---

*Insulating concrete forms (ICFs) are Styrofoam forms into which a builder pours concrete. They have a very high insulation value.

**SIPs (structural insulated panels) are wall sections made from a recycled plywood product laminated onto Styrofoam. They are an incredibly energy- and materials-efficient way to build and are widely and successfully used.

MR. CONTRACTOR: That stuff is a bunch of hogwash you don't need and we never put anything like that in.

MR. GREEN: Please recycle your beer cans and wood while drinking and working on our job site.

MR. CONTRACTOR: Yeah, cool, okay. Bottles and cans, clap your hands. (*Everyone's on board with that one.*)

"It goes on from there. A contractor can always trump an owner who wants to go green because any builder knows an order of magnitude more than an owner. The owner doesn't know what to do because he's not the expert.

"I see the contractors as a huge piece in the equation who in my opinion have the most control in implementing this stuff (other than code pricks and DRB [design review board] Nazis).*

"Who am I to argue with them? They're the experts in the field, they know what they're doing. So you get talked out of it. What started out as a green structure turns into something status quo, and maybe you get lucky and use a little Trex (a recycled plastic faux-wood product) on the deck.

"Contractors have little if any incentive to build any differently than they do now. They don't live in these houses or pay for the heating bills. They've made good money doing

---

*At best, DRBs protect the common good of the community by preventing people from doing things on their property that harm the neighborhood or (God forbid) lower resale values of surrounding properties. At worst, they trample over personal property rights, add red tape, and eliminate individualism and character so that every street looks the same except for the name—the epitome of tract development. DRBs also have a tendency to ban clotheslines.

what they do, they do it well, and anything that changes or threatens that throws in a level of uncertainty and concern. Hey, building houses is hard work, dealing with bitchy homeowners who want their frickin' travertine slab counters and endless pool system in before Christmas, DRBs, code zealots, substandard or never-available subcontractors, and climate change–induced chaotic weather patterns.

"Educating homeowners is key, but the hard part is we're programmed to buy the chrome package instead of paying attention to what's under the hood. Starchitects* are building monuments to their, and their owners', egos. Even if you did care, there's no sticker on the window when you move in that tells you your miles per gallon. When I talk to folks about R-values, thermal mass, boiler efficiencies, and air infiltration, their eyes glaze over. Dumb it down too much and you come up with some crappy pie chart in *USA Today* that says I can save the planet by turning down my thermostat and having someone look at my furnace to make sure it's running right. I have to admit that, even though on our own house we're stoked to be able to do some good stuff, when I drive by a home built wrong but reasonably priced (is that possible?), it would be nice to just be able to move into something and not go through all the brain damage.

"This is where a green building code for the whole community works and comes in as a win-win. Just raise the bar and make it required. Contractors then would know how to

----

*An architect with a large ego or reputation for outlandish designs. Frank Gehry, for example.

build to code and know what to expect and how to do it. Homeowners get a code-certified green building with better indoor air quality, and it saves them money with little additional up-front costs or headaches. The community and environment benefit collectively from improved material use and reduced emissions. Egotects* are happy because there's still plenty of innovation and creativity built into the code so they can come up with the latest eco-design and get written up in all the fancy magazines even if in the real world their design sucks."

Whew! Adam's commentary is the dark side of the new-construction business. But it points to the need for broad standards—codes—that level the playing field so that the guy who wants to go green is business as usual instead of some outlying weirdo. Changing building codes is one of the best things we can do to address climate change, period.

Retrofitting Your Grandmother's House

New construction is just a piece of the building challenge—there's a dark side to the *remodel* business, too, and remembering Mazria, we have to fix existing buildings if we want a prayer of solving climate change. There are millions of hogs like the one I'm typing this in throughout the United States, the vast majority built to very lame energy efficiency standards. So what's our problem? Let's get on it! Yet in this arena, too, there are significant barriers. As David Roberts has

....
*Architects.

pointed out on Grist.org, "With today's technology, we know how to make new buildings net energy generators, and we know how to retrofit existing buildings to reduce their energy consumption by well over 50%, in some cases 90–95%. We just need someone to pay for it." Roberts notes that investment in such retrofits has three main features: (1) it is capital-intensive up front (with huge labor costs); (2) it pays off slowly and modestly; and (3) it's a sure thing in terms of eventual savings. "Hypercapitalism being what it is . . . investors are heavily predisposed against investments with features 1 and 2."[7]

Environmental Building News reported in July 2007 that there were 124 million housing units in the United States, ignoring commercial buildings. These units used 21 percent of the energy in the United States, or 36 percent of total electricity consumption. That accounts for 330 million metric tons of carbon. We have to fix these buildings, too!

In the same way that we need an outside entity to offer cash to "prime the pump" for business efficiency programs, fixing old buildings, as Roberts points out, seems to be an obvious role for government. "Figuring out financing mechanisms for such investments is a public policy with guaranteed payback, considerable social benefit, and built in political support—a gimme."

We need such a mechanism at Aspen Skiing Company. The planet may be warming, but where I work, our bean counters are freezing. Downstairs in the finance department, every single person in a dozen offices and cubicles has at least one inefficient electric space heater on, all winter long. I have seen our CFO typing in fingerless gloves. Why? Our office building's heating system doesn't work so well, at least not down there. (Other parts of the building are too hot.) In one room the heat was stuck on for a month—in the summer.

This situation may sound like an unfortunate inconvenience, and you might be thinking that I should stop whining. But it's nothing so trivial. This building—with our grumpy and cold accountants, our overheating marketing team, and Barb at the front desk with the door open and the heat on (not her fault)—represents ground zero of the climate wars; our very future depends on fixing buildings just like this one.

Here's the problem: *It's viciously difficult.* Here in the Aspen Skiing Company office building, for example, we *have* "gotten on it." We've been trying to fix this thirty-year-old pig for four years now. And we've found that the cost of the fix, using any rational financial metrics, is outrageous and offers little to no return on investment. It's hard for a variety of reasons. Engineers disagree on the correct fix: Each one has a different perspective. Who's right? Sticker shock causes managers like me to approve multiple Band-Aid solutions instead of more complete fixes. Simultaneously, more critical projects—like replacing broken water pipes and fixing leaky roofs—may be competing for the pool of money we'd use. As a result, we find ourselves limping along, trying to make it another year, rather than spending the $250,000 to $500,000 it would take to make everyone comfortable and save some (but not all that much) energy.

But wait: We're a motivated company with a track record that, if we say so ourselves, puts us at the forefront of the sustainability movement. *And yet we're having trouble fixing just one of our 250 existing buildings.* How is the world, which operates on a fixed setting of "business as usual," going to deal with this overwhelming challenge?

The short story is that it isn't going to happen—we aren't going to solve the challenge of existing buildings and, consequently, the climate problem—without a comprehensive national program to finance the work. We need such a program—cobbled together through government, nonprofit, and foundation funding and called, say, Priming the Pump for Buildings—because right now only the most ethical and motivated individuals and companies are doing anything, and the vast majority of building owners are sitting on their hands. We need a program that literally pays for a portion of these retrofits, donating cash so that the return on investment becomes acceptable, or at least so the price of the fix isn't prohibitive.

This program has to happen soon—almost instantly. When I say that scientists are telling us we have a decade to replace the inefficient infrastructure that is hobbling our climate, they are speaking in part about our buildings—about the building you're sitting in right now. More practically, I'm worried that our finance department is going to quit en masse if we don't do something, and fast.

In fact, progressive governments and foundations are already moving in this direction. Cambridge, Massachusetts, thanks to a grant and leadership from the Kendall Foundation (a remarkable organization that has creatively taken on climate change as a jihad), started a program to finance just such efficiency work in buildings. And Berkeley, California, now loans homeowners money to install solar panels. Homeowners pay the loan back over twenty years through an almost unnoticeable property tax increase, and the city makes a modest profit.

Resistance to Change Is Endemic

Five years ago, Aspen Skiing Company started designing some new luxury condominiums in Snowmass Village. The condos would be above eight thousand feet, so air conditioning should not have been necessary. But during early meetings with the design team, it became clear that "full climate control" would be installed. I was incredulous. Why would we install air conditioning this high in the Rocky Mountains, where temperatures rarely get uncomfortable and we could design buildings that provided comfort without AC?

"We understand that," the project managers said. "But in this high-end market, you simply can't sell this product without full climate control." From an energy standpoint, this appeared to be a checkmate. Air conditioning is very energy-intensive.

If we're going to solve the climate challenge, we're going to have to replace energy with an even scarcer resource—intelligence. And in fact, in the case of the Snowmass condos, we were able to do that. A member of the design team, after pondering this problem, noticed that there was a lake (actually, a tertiary sewage treatment pond) not far from the condos. Why not use that relatively warm water as a heat sink to heat the buildings in the winter and cool them in summer? The mechanical system he was proposing is called a pond-source heat pump, and it works on the same principle as your basement. Because the ground temperature is a constant fifty-seven degrees year-round, your basement feels cool in summer and relatively warm in winter. The same relatively constant temperature exists in a pond. And pond-source, or ground-source, heat pumps are not new technology: They've been around for almost a century.* Such systems typically cut the energy use in a building by half right off the bat.

We ended up designing the Sanctuary condos with this system, which circulates a food-grade propylene glycol solution through a series of coils in the pond.

When we fired up the system . . . there were lots of problems. The project manager came to me with the standard complaint: "See, we tried something new, and we had all these problems. . . . " But ask any project manager if the system worked perfectly at first on his last business-as-usual project. The answer is, "Of course not." So why should green building be held to higher standards? Because it's green.

After the system was commissioned, it worked as well as a conventional system. In fact, we installed the same system

---

*"Ground source" systems like this are, generally speaking, the same technology as a *cave*, which is why caves were the first housing for humans, even before humans were human.

for a nearby golf clubhouse that achieved LEED Silver. But both systems remain under close scrutiny.

Why is change so hard? When I ask someone why they did something a particular way and the response is, "That's how we've always done it," my gut reaction has always been, "What a dumb answer." But there's a reason the old guys in an organization do things like they do, and there's a reason change is hard: the status quo *works*, and change is sometimes inconvenient, painful, or even mistaken. You have to understand this before you can overcome it.

Looking for a Few Good Men and Women

So what's the solution?

In short—leadership and talent. As a building owner, you have to recognize what's important—energy efficiency—and insist on it, not settle for a decent LEED rating but lousy energy performance. It is sooooooo easy to respond to an engineer who says, "It's too expensive to do 50 percent energy efficiency . . . will you settle for 20?" with a sigh and an "Okay." Instead, to quote Winston Churchill, you must "never give in. Never. Never. Never. Never."[8] And if you fail, instead of telling the world about your green rating, talk about why and how you failed. Yes, that's going to be scary and embarrassing, and it might even seem damaging to your business. But it won't be. Talking about your mistakes will prove your transparency and honesty and only help the larger cause.

At the same time, you have to have the right people working with you. Yes, there is a famous building in Zimbabwe called Eastgate that looks like a cactus and as a result self-shades and dumps heat. But the building isn't successful because it looks like a saguaro or breathes like a termite mound and some manager didn't have a miracle pitch to get people to act, plan, and work differently. It's successful because the owners insisted on high performance, and the architect, Mick Pearce, who is now applying his magic in Melbourne, is a genius. And there's the rub. Successful green buildings depend on qualified green engineers, architects, and builders led by owners who demand nothing less than radical energy efficiency. But since people with this level of experience, talent, and leadership ability are in short supply, homeowners inevitably go through the following process:

> Hire a business-as-usual architect who is someone you know and like from working together before, but who has no green building experience.

> Hire a business-as-usual mechanical engineer—in other words, a firm dedicated to covering its rear and therefore overengineering the HVAC system.

> Now try to jerry-rig the already doomed process by tweaking it or by spending even more money on a green consultant to whom well-intentioned owners ascribe God-like qualities.

Make a few tweaks but fail to do anything very different from business as usual and end up with a code-built structure, like many new LEED-certified buildings. Cut most of the progressive stuff in the "value engineering" phase. Call the project "green" even though it's mediocre.

Declare victory, knowing that you've utterly failed, and worse, that you've created a "successful blueprint" for future failure. Go to confession.

Don't share your mistakes with anyone. In fact, live in fear that they'll be found out. Leave the country.

Ultimately, we need to find a way to make green building more accessible. A construction manager once asked me: "What's the process we go through to make a green building?" (His first question was: "What's green building?") I should have been able to hand him a one-pager, but I didn't have one. Each project manager needs to be able to articulate the process clearly and quickly.

Here's how it *should* work, from an owner's perspective:

Hire skilled architects, engineers, and contractors who are all committed to the cause. They don't have to be green. But they do have to understand that they work for you and you are paying them to build a green building within budget.

Provide a roadmap that describes the process and goals for building green. (More on that roadmap later.)

Make sure there is a project champion, preferably a bulldog, to hound people. Stay vigilant throughout the whole process.

When the project is finished, share your successes, but also share the inevitable pitfalls with others—internally, at conferences, and through other outlets like writing books and magazine articles and posting on Web sites.

Make your next building even better.

Even if you do all this, the problem of bringing together subcontractors who don't know each other and don't necessarily share the same mission is a problem we may never escape. As Randy Udall points out, "If the ski industry worked like the building industry, you'd contract with a snow removal outfitter to groom the slopes, ski patrol would be hired each morning on a street corner, marketing would be outsourced to India, etc. Instead, you guys are vertically integrated top to bottom. What happened to the construction industry?" And as Amory Lovins has said, if the auto industry ran like the construction industry, it would have gone out of business long ago.

A Path Forward

There are some other steps we can take moving forward. The first step is to change green building conferences so that they're useful. Right now, they're an aggregation of consultants, architects, planners, builders, and engineers trying to get work by showcasing their projects. All participants are motivated to avoid admitting mistakes. (Can you imagine an architect getting up and saying: "Boy, did we screw up this building. Let me tell you about it. . . .") Instead, conference organizers should mostly invite speakers who are willing to get into the nitty-gritty of the building process and talk about how to do it better, in the process exposing their mistakes and teaching people how to avoid them. In short, we need honest discussions, not sales jobs.

Second, we need to focus on the ability and motivation of contractors. You can't make a green building with unwilling or unskilled team members, but that's what we're doing most of the time. At most businesses, Aspen Skiing Company being no exception, it is very hard to move away from the tried-and-true business-as-usual architects and take a flyer on a green designer who may be either new or based out of state. To be fair, a green designer can represent a real risk with real potential costs. At the same time, building is a very human endeavor. You pick an architect (as we have done at Aspen Skiing Company) because you know him or her, because you kayak together, or because you owe that person a business favor. That is reality. But you can't take talentless or ignorant architects and engineers and hope that a green design process will make the project green. It won't happen. But we've found that if you get a good architect who understands green design, you're halfway there; if you get a mechanical engineer who knows and cares about efficiency on board as well, you're done.

Third, we need to focus on changing codes, particularly energy efficiency requirements. This is already happening in many progressive municipalities. Aspen and Crested Butte are two Colorado examples. Changing commercial and residential codes, in one sweep of the pen, does more good than centuries of piecemeal green building. Moving the power and spotlight of LEED toward codes is one way to get the big-picture change we need now.

We also need to invest in implementing solutions. Alex Wilson at *Environmental Building News* has suggested that, given the scope and scale of the problem, we need an "Environmental Service Corps" for America, a cross between FDR's New Deal Civilian Conservation Corps and Kennedy's Peace Corps. It would, according to Wilson, "ask men and women to invest two years of their lives in the service of their country, especially after high school or college—by carrying out a wide range of projects to help our nation reduce the likelihood of catastrophic climate change while at the same time adapting to changes brought about by climate change."[9] Wilson extends the idea beyond work on buildings and into critical projects like ecological restoration and reforestation. He is dead on. This would be a corps of climate soldiers, protecting the planet for their children by doing something like that nasty job I had just out of college: energy technician. Is the investment too much?

I think almost any price would be reasonable. Stephen Schneider, the Stanford-based climate scientist, has pointed out that faced with the cold war—a problem that had a low risk of happening but high consequences (a U.S.-Soviet nuclear war)—we threw billions and billons of dollars at the problem. Yet faced with the problem of climate change, which has a 100 percent chance of happening (it's actually occurring) and equally dire consequences that are more or less inevitable, we've barely mobilized. And we've barely mobilized because our leaders tell us it would be too hard on the economy to do so. But as Harvard's John Holdren has pointed out, we didn't delay the war on terrorism because it would be too costly.[10]

Finally, we need to find a way to make green building more accessible to the masses.

LEED is an attempt at that, but it has the boomerang problem of appearing to be a secret language. And since LEED is a certification system—not a roadmap—our best approach is to ignore LEED until we're done with the building. Once the building is finished, we can see what we've got—and then by all means certify. That keeps us honest and prevents the certification program from driving the process. Better still would be a USGBC-sanctioned "LEED Construction Process"—a manual for green building, from floor plans to roof shingles.

Make Love—Heat the House

Ultimately, the success or failure of the green building movement may hinge on how good we are at being teachers, not builders. It's much easier to go through a LEED checklist than to show someone how to build a green building. But it's much more interesting and valuable (and fun!) when designers or builders tell war stories.

A man named Jack Aley used to guest-lecture to environmental studies classes at Bowdoin College when I was a student there. He talked about the house he had built in coastal Maine. Throughout the presentation, he always returned to one theme: "Simple and elegant. Passive solar! Face it south! Superinsulation! Thermal mass. It's simple, it's elegant." Jack heated his house with a small woodstove, but he said it was so tight you could heat the place by making love. Jack boiled down this confusing field of green building to a few shouted words.

A Redneck Ten Commandments

Frank and forthright, brusque and loud, Jack is a classic Maine straight shooter even though he's from Illinois and was educated at Dartmouth. And maybe that's what we need most of all to complement our integrated processes and biomimicry and LEED and life-cycle analysis: a painfully candid, redneck ten commandments of green building.

1. Don't bother with green building unless you have a committed owner, sufficient time, and a good project manager.
2. Focus on talent: Hire the best goddamn engineer you can find, a committed architect, and a construction company that believes.
3. Have a good bullshit detector: Accept no compromises or excuses.
4. Screw consultants.
5. Forget the fruit salad (certification) until you're done—then use it to see how you did.
6. Don't forget the subcontractors—they are the ground troops.
7. Keep your eye on the ball, which is energy efficiency, not bamboo floors.
8. Don't fall in love with renewables or funky ecoproducts, and save biomimicry for tomorrow. For today, just get 'er done right.
9. Superinsulate, caulk, and face it south.
10. Be paranoid: commission it.*

And number 11, the redneck equivalent of commissioning, at least for residential construction: If you can heat the house by making love, you done good.

---

*Commissioning, discussed in Chapter 5, is a third-party inspection of the heating system to make sure you did it right.

A Coda on Green Building

For all the barriers and obstacles, pitfalls and potholes on the path to widespread adoption of green building practices, this field is slowly taking root, even among the most jaded and traditionalist of contractors. It is impossible not to be excited as greenness blossoms in many forms throughout the built environment, even if you still can't buy a green home in the average subdivision.

I caught a glimpse of this light—the palpable spread of the green movement in building—at what was one of the lowest points in my green building career. In November 2007, a team of Aspen Skiing Company project managers were on the verge of completing a remodel of a sixty-bed affordable housing project in Aspen called the Holiday House. The project was unique because we had taken a crappy old lodge and radically refurbished it, making it a model for green design. Better still, the sustainability department, which I run, had effectively had nothing to do with the project, other than finding the money for a solar system to be installed after completion. This was an indicator of how broadly the green ethic had spread within the company.

Before Mark Vogele and Bill Boyd took on the project, the structure missed the local energy code by 80 percent. After they blew highly insulating foam into the walls and roof, installed krypton gas–filled windows that insulated four times as well as conventional models, revamped the heating system, and put in efficient appliances and water heaters, the new building beat energy code by 20 percent—a swing of one hundred percentage points in energy efficiency.

It is not hyperbolic to say that efforts like this one to fix old buildings will be the tangible work of our generation more than any other climate solution, in the same way that homesteading was the work of Americans in the 1850s, or defeating Hitler was the job of the twentieth century's "greatest generation." Solar and other renewable technologies, appliance efficiency, and carbon taxation will all happen in the realm of policy, government, and big business. But all Americans will somehow have to engage in the task of fixing the places they live in, using their own hands and some of their own money.

Shortly before completion, on a crisp and clear November night, the Holiday House caught fire and burned to the ground.

Because so many had so much invested in the project, I wrote an e-mail sending my condolences to several of the project managers. Here's the response I got from David Corbin, Aspen Skiing Company's vice president of planning:

> Thanks for the thoughts and condolences. Seeing the building burn down after all the hard work to get it started was a heartbreaking thing to watch. Re-running the building permit gauntlet is cause for prolonged grief. But, we will do it again.
>
> You would be pleased to know that among the subcontractors called back to the site last night were a couple of

rough around the edges builder types who were actually commenting to one another that they were sorry to see the building burn because this was the first real green building they'd worked on and they thought that was a cool thing. The green building ethic is slowly spreading into the full breadth of the construction industry. Life is interesting.

NINE

Shameless Self-Promotion
and Why It Matters

Those who tell the stories rule society.

—PLATO

Climate change is the defining problem of our time. Even George Bush, who has long denied the problem (or admitted the problem but denied the need to take action), started to come around: He finally mentioned the words "climate change" in a State of the Union message in 2007 and organized a summit on the subject a year before he left office. (Nothing came of it.) The prime minister of Australia—the only other major Western nation that didn't sign Kyoto—was dramatically and overwhelmingly ousted in 2007, in large part because of his climate stance. And other unusual suspects, like Rex Tillerson, the CEO of ExxonMobil, which has spent years and millions of dollars funding misinformation campaigns against climate action, are changing their tune: Tillerson recently renounced the company's years of denial and its funding for denial.[1]

And yet, just as the media frenzy over climate change and greenness in general seemed to be reaching a point of sustained apex, a member of another company's marketing department approached me with this question: "I know that global warming is all the rage right now, but what's the next thing? What's going to be big next year?" I was speechless. Climate change is not like camo in the eighties, a passing fad. Nevertheless, climate change is still not on people's radar, despite the incredible scientific evidence and media storm, as a problem of "transcendent urgency," as writer Bill McKibben has called it. Why?

When you go home to your in-laws' house for dinner in Oklahoma and the dinner table conversation turns to climate change, almost invariably Uncle Frank says, "Isn't there some doubt about the science?" As we saw in Chapter 2, it's not that there's any doubt. "Consensus" might be a bad word, since it suggests a bunch of liberals in a room conspiring, so think instead of the thousands of scientists all over the world, doing research on their own, using different methodologies in different places, speaking different languages and espousing different ideologies, who are all coming up with the same conclusions—the earth is warming and humans are the cause. Anthropogenic warming just happens to be the case. Russian ice core drillers in Greenland just happen to agree with the Americans doing the same thing in Antarctica.

Uncle Frank's skepticism stems in large part from the great marketing success of ExxonMobil, which, according to a 2005 report in *Mother Jones* magazine (later confirmed by ExxonMobil itself), has funded at least "40 organizations that either have sought to undermine mainstream scientific findings on global climate change or have maintained affiliations with a small group of 'skeptic' scientists who continue to do so. Beyond think tanks, [ExxonMobil has funded] quasi-journalistic outlets like TechcentralStation.com (a website providing 'news, analysis, research, and commentary' that received $95,000 from ExxonMobil in 2003), a FoxNews.com columnist, and even religious and civil rights groups. In total, these organizations received more than $8 million between 2000 and 2003."[2] And that was just the tip of the iceberg. Not just ExxonMobil but many others in the coal and oil business have been funding disinformation campaigns for years.

Al Gore's Alliance for Climate Protection will spend $300 million over the next three years on a marketing campaign designed to get Americans to address climate change. Why, though? Shouldn't he be working to cut carbon dioxide emissions?

Marketing green is important because it's becoming increasingly clear that climate change may indeed be primarily a PR and marketing problem. As Gore understands, we're not going to create the societal will for World War II–scale action on climate change without a major countermarketing campaign. We came to the same conclusion here at Aspen Skiing Company. Marketing was another of our big levers.

In an attempt to speed up the cultural change our society needs to go through—and to reach that generally wealthy and influential audience, our guests—we launched an ad campaign focused on climate change called "Save Snow," which featured a beautiful, powder-filled mountain bowl with a melting snowflake superimposed on it. The text read:

SNOW: CERTIFICATE OF DEATH

Full Name: Snow. Nicknames(s): Powder, Freshies, Blower. Age at Death: Timeless. Appearance: White, Cold. Medical History: Ailing Since the Dawn of the Industrial Age. Events Leading to Death: Global warming Pollution, Blatant Disregard for Climate Change. Suspects(s): Humanity. Cause of Death: Ignorance, Indifference.

Aspen/Snowmass experienced near record snowfall last season. Not surprisingly, we want to keep it that way. Join our movement to SAVE SNOW at www.savesnow.org.

The point of the ads was multifold. First, the goal from a purely advertising standpoint was to separate Aspen Skiing Company from the pack. All ski resort ads, and all articles on skiing, look exactly the same, featuring a well-dressed skier floating through several feet of powder on a blue-sky day. Anything different would stand out. Second, we wanted to activate the skiing base with an educational Web site featuring world-class skiers and snowboarders and a climate message focused on political action. The Web site directs visitors to write their congresspeople and get engaged in an effort to drive policy change. Finally, the ad campaign was trying to address, and counter, the sad reality that action on climate policy has been woefully slow in part because of marketing from the denier community (like the ExxonMobil work).

Aspen Skiing Company's ad campaign is an effort to fight fire with fire, to throw marketing dollars at the problem in a way that is good for business and good for the climate. Because it's not enough to put your head down and work—you have to get others on board and spread the word.

There is a pitfall, however, to this kind of promotion. The second you do something like this, or talk about your environmental work more broadly, you're subject to accusations of environmental disingenuity or hypocrisy, also known as "greenwashing."

Greenwashing Is Good for the Environment (. . . If You Get Caught)

Greenwashing is bad in that it's deceitful. But if we're going to be purely Machiavellian about saving the planet, greenwashing might not be all that bad for the environment itself, never mind the ethics.

To greenwash, according to Word Spy, a Web site dedicated to new words and phrases, is "to implement token environmentally friendly initiatives as a way of hiding or deflecting criticism about existing environmentally destructive practices." But greenwashing also means outright deception. Calling a timber-harvesting program "Healthy Forests"? Greenwash. Calling a pollution reduction program that has been roundly condemned by environmental groups "Clear

Skies"? Greenwash. An automaker that opposes stricter fuel-efficiency standards pledging in full-page *New York Times* ads to reduce greenhouse gas emissions? Greenwash.

Early on at Aspen Skiing Company, we decided that the only way to spread the word about our environmental work and drive change in the industry and beyond would be to promote our work widely, through articles, PR, and interviews, fears of being accused of greenwashing notwithstanding.

In public talks about Aspen Skiing Company's environmental programs, I used to describe our wind-powered Cirque chairlift. Renewable-energy purchases for that lift keep thirty thousand pounds of carbon dioxide, the primary greenhouse gas, out of the air annually, I'd tell my audience. Furthermore, it was the first renewably powered lift in the country.

My listeners would often applaud the accomplishment. But then I'd tell them they had been greenwashed.

The next thing I'd say was that the Cirque lift constituted .00454 percent of our total electricity requirements. It was our first step in a renewable power plan that eventually brought total wind power purchases (from non-REC sources) to 2 percent, then to 6 percent, and, if all goes well, to 100 percent by 2011. That's not a bad effort for an energy-intensive business like skiing. But with the Cirque, the initial purchase of wind energy could have been called insignificant tokenism, because it wasn't backed by a grand plan. The Cirque story illustrates just how difficult it is to be a consumer and a business in the age of environmental awareness. While consumers need to be constantly on the alert for potential greenwash, businesses need them to be

willing to recognize—and applaud—genuine efforts to protect the environment.

Still, if greenwashing is ethically questionable and probably exposes businesses to increased scrutiny and criticism,
why are so many doing it?

The answer is that they sniff an emerging trend. In theory,
U.S. consumers will increasingly be taking into account the environmental and social impacts of products and manufacturers.
According to the journal *Lifestyles of Health and Sustainability*,
in 2000 the LOHAS market represented $546 billion globally
and $226.8 billion in the United States. That's a big market if
it ever decides to start acting on principle. Meanwhile, for businesses like oil companies that require local and government approval for exploration, a green image provides a "license to
operate." If drilling is inevitable, why not give the contract to
the oil company that has a green reputation?

Unfortunately, it's not always clear who's greenwashing
and who's for real.

In his book *The Corporate Planet*, Joshua Karliner lam-
bastes DuPont for a public relations campaign that featured
"an ad full of seals clapping, whales and dolphins jumping,
and flamingos flying, all set to Beethoven's Ode to Joy, to
project its newfound green image."[3] But DuPont arguably is
a green company that has already met a target to reduce
greenhouse gas emissions 65 percent by 2010 (based on a
1990 baseline). That's nothing to sneeze at, and DuPont has
many fans in the environmental community.

Meanwhile, in the 1990s, Shell set a new low in corporate
environmental responsibility when Ken Saro-Wiwa, the

Nigerian writer, was executed for protesting the company's exploration in Africa.[4] Shell undertook a massive social and environmental responsibility PR campaign in response to boycotts. In 2001, CorpWatch reported that Shell "continues its clever but misleading ad series 'Profits or Principles' which touts Shell's commitment to renewable energy sources and features photos of lush green forests. But Shell spends a minuscule 0.6 percent of its annual investments on renewables."[5] Today, although the company has invested in renewable energy resources and a few years ago launched an ad campaign touting the greenness of its fuel, its troubles in Nigeria and other areas continue. Research suggests that Shell still might not be all it claims. Same with fellow oil company BP, which changed its name from British Petroleum to "Beyond Petroleum." In 2007 the company announced that it would invest $3 billion in Canadian oil sands, the dirtiest of all fuels, and one of the planet's great ecological catastrophes. (Shell, too, has joined the Canadian oil sands debacle.)

The mother of all recent greenwashing comes from GM, which launched a national advertising campaign in the fall of 2007 in major magazines like the *New Yorker* and *Wired*. The campaign, which features full-page ads of sunlit spiderwebs, accompanied by pullout booklets, reads as follows:

> Everyone can appreciate technologies that go from gas-friendly to gas-free. That's why Chevy offers eight 2007 models that get 30 mpg highway or better, plus more vehicle choices today than any brand that run on cleaner-

burning, mostly renewable E85 ethanol. It's also why, this fall, we'll offer both Malibu Hybrid and Tahoe Hybrid—America's first full-size hybrid SUV. And why we've put tremendous design and engineering resources in place to make Concept Chevy Volt—our extended-range electric vehicle—a reality. Now that's technology everyone can appreciate. Do more. Use less. Find out how at chevy.com. An American Revolution.[6]

The greenwashing, if not already apparent, becomes clear when you read the little booklet. The first page is on fuel efficiency. Regardless of what the company says on this front, it's well known that GM strongly opposed, and continues to oppose, federal increases in vehicle mileage standards (along with perceived green leaders like Toyota). And even if that weren't problematic enough, the cars that GM brags about—the Silverado and Tahoe—get 14 miles per gallon in the city and 21 on the highway. For reference, the Model T got between 25 and 30 miles per gallon. And U.S. average fleet fuel economy is 21 miles per gallon.

Turn the page—GM talks about E85 ethanol. A truck that runs on E85 is no different, and no more efficient, than a non-flex-fuel truck. And Ford, which isn't a green company either, has been making them for close to a decade. Turn the page again and you get to the Chevy Volt, an electric car you can't buy as of the writing of this book. Turn the page again and you're reading about GM's fuel cell work. Fuel cells in vehicles, if they're a viable technology at all, are probably twenty years out. That's part of the reason the Bush administration targeted so much attention on fuel cells: They wouldn't have to do anything about this technology during their term of office.

As this advertising campaign reached a peak, General Motors' vice chairman Bob Lutz told reporters in January 2008 that global warming is a "total crock of shit."[7] He later qualified that statement by saying: "I'm a skeptic, not a denier."

Lutz also said that hybrid cars like the Toyota Prius "make no economic sense" because their price will never come down, and that diesel cars like those being marketed by Chrysler are also uneconomical.

Finally, the last page of the booklet is titled "Some Things We Can All Do Right Now to Help the Planet." One of those suggestions is to stop using phone books. At this point, if you're not gagging, you're employed by GM. When a dying person tells you he feels great and is going to live forever, you don't contradict him, because it's too sad and it's pointless anyway. So it goes with GM, a dying company.*

Nonetheless, and counterintuitively, greenwash—real or perceived—can actually be good for the environment, if not a business's reputation for honesty. As soon as a company starts hyping its environmental responsibility, legitimately or not, it creates enormous pressure to follow through. It invites greater scrutiny from the public, the press, employees, and watchdog groups. Activating employees alone is a huge change agent. If a company isn't living up to the standard it sets publicly, em-

----

*To its credit, GM is retooling the company around the Volt, the plug-in hybrid. That's encouraging. But also, arguably, too late.

ployees will complain, and they'll work to change their company, because nobody likes to work for a cheat.

At Aspen Skiing Company, many of our new program
ideas come from irate callers who say, "You're not as green as
you say—you're not (fill in the blank: recycling properly,
revegetating your slopes, addressing snowmaking issues)."
Often callers have good ideas and we implement them.
Would we receive those calls had we not declared ourselves
green? Painting a business green inevitably steers it toward
improved practices.

If we do something good at Aspen Skiing Company—
like powering our snowcats with clean, renewable biodiesel
until U.S. diesel standards get better, or building a snow-
boarding halfpipe out of dirt to save water—we always send
out a press release, because we believe the public and other
businesses need to know what's possible. In fact, by being
leaders in ski-area environmentalism and making a big deal
out of it, Aspen Skiing Company has arguably forced the rest
of the industry to change, maybe even helped create an arms
race. If we stayed humble and quiet, other resorts wouldn't
feel pressed to compete.

If firms are afraid to hype their good environmental projects because they fear being labeled greenwashers, nothing
will change. Information on business as usual is already out
there. Progressive new green information is not. Getting the
word out, with the hope of changing the world, is worth the
risk.

An official at a neighboring (and rival) ski resort once
commented, in response to our own consistent and shameless

promotion of our environmental work, "We don't need to do a press release every time we do a lighting retrofit." I believe this is incorrect. You do need to issue the press release, for two reasons: your mission and your business. Because we need *everyone* on board with a climate action program. This should be every company's perspective, unless your mission is global warming.

How does this help business? Our environmental work has been covered in *Time*, *Outside*, *Newsweek*, and *Business Week* and by CNBC and scores of other media outlets. Our PR department puts cash value on "placements" of the Aspen/Snowmass brand. *Time* alone was worth about $100,000. *Business Week* was valued at over $1 million.

Your Motivation for Going Green Is Irrelevant . . . as Long as You're Doing It

In the sustainability field, we talk about businesses that are motivated to address climate change by profit, return on investment, better worker productivity, and so forth. Managers who espouse these incentives are seen as visionary, progressive, and "deep green." But businesses and individuals are often afraid to say that their green efforts have a profit motive behind them.

There is a persistent feeling in our culture that individuals and corporations should undertake environmental work out of the goodness of their hearts. Workers in the environmental movement should be underpaid, and the only reason for doing green work is that "it's the right thing to do." What we hear is that it's not just the end result that matters, it's the motivation for doing the work that got you there. But motivation shouldn't matter. In fact, the idea that our motivations must be pure or our actions will be inauthentic and therefore corrupt and meaningless is one of the great myths of the green movement.

When I worked as an ambulance medic, I often encountered "trauma junkies." These were other medics who just loved the "good" (bad) calls—the serious car wrecks, the mass casualty incidents. These folks lived for these events, trained for them, probably dreamed about them. At first, I scoffed. What ghouls, what weirdos. But over time, working with the trauma junkies, I began to wonder: *Who would I want to take care of me if I were in an accident?* And the answer was: the person who lives and breathes disaster.

In some cases, people's motivation for what they do is irrelevant, as long as the outcome is good. If a desire for free publicity, or glory, or self-aggrandizement motivates individuals or companies to go green, why shouldn't they promote themselves ruthlessly? Given the climate crisis, we can't afford to squander any opportunity, or any motivation, to both enact change and create a broader conversation about that change. In fact, if solutions to the climate problem were driven by greed, wouldn't that be the best possible outcome?

Do Customers Care?

Still, a niggling question, at least from a pure business perspective, is whether anyone cares. Does green marketing, greenwash or not, actually do anything for your business? This question is especially hard to answer given that there is limited empirical evidence that being green, or having a green product, helps anyone sell product or thrive as a business. An infamous *Wall Street Journal* article by Geoffrey Fowler in 2002, titled "'Green' Sales Pitch Isn't Moving Many Products," pointed out that "shoppers will pay for convenience far more readily than for ideology."[8] The article noted that after years and years of green marketing efforts, businesses—at least in 2002—were seeing declining interest or benefit from green branding.

In 2003, Cait Murphy pointed out in *Fortune* magazine something that appears to hold true today: "The message . . . is that for business to make money out of greenery requires a steely-eyed recognition of reality—that people do not and will not weigh the social, ethical, and environmental consequences of every purchasing decision. . . . The Toronto-based International Institute for Sustainable Development figures that no more than 2% of North American consumers are 'deep green'—that is, willing to seek out and pay for environmentally superior products."[9]

The trend continues to this day. A 2006 study by Landor Associates in New York found that 64 percent of respondents couldn't name a "green" brand.[10] Over half of those who considered themselves green were unable to name one. "As much as the term has been tossed around, many people . . . are unclear as to what it means," the study reported. "Eco-friendly, fuel efficient, biodegradable, natural and organic are used in different categories to emphasize green, but can confuse and cloud the mind of consumers."

In 2007, Yankelovich, a well-respected consumer research company that's been around since 1958, released a new study of Americans' buying habits.[11] The study found that 37 percent of consumers are "highly concerned" about the environment, but that only 25 percent feel that they are highly knowledgeable about environmental issues. And only 22 percent think they can make a difference.

The president of Yankelovich, Walker Smith, summed up the study: "Given consumer attitudes today, green is best characterized as a niche opportunity in the consumer marketplace. It is a strong niche opportunity, but it is not a mainstream interest that is passionately held or strongly felt by the majority of consumers. . . . The majority of consumers don't care all that much about the environment. Green simply hasn't captured the public imagination."

This may seem hard to believe, since every single major magazine has, more than once, devoted cover stories to the subject of green in general or climate change in particular. Rock stars, actors, and pro athletes are talking about it, and most Fortune 500 companies either have green programs or are working on them. Al Gore won a Nobel, and Wal-Mart is selling hundreds of thousands of compact fluorescent bulbs for under $2.

But, the study reveals, media attention doesn't track with consumer attitudes. In commenting on this gap, Joel Makower, a well-known green business writer and strategist, noted in his blog "Two Steps Up" that 82 percent of Americans have neither read nor seen Al Gore's book and movie *An Inconvenient Truth*. And Walker Smith points out that "the amount of media interest given to the environment far exceeds the amount of consumer interest."

The bottom line: most executives would have a hard time making a strong case for green brand positioning to a CFO—at least, if they were trying to base their case on empirical evidence.

But they're spending lots of money on it anyway. Why?

The reason seems to be twofold: One, they see a big emerging market. Increasing evidence, including surveys of our own customers, shows that even if awareness is now generally low, interest in the greenness of a business (and willingness to spend more on green products) is growing exponentially, even if people are not necessarily making decisions on what they buy based on that criterion.

For example, Chris Wilson, president of Experian Research Service, says that "it is believed that green consumers will have an estimated annual buying power of up to $500 billion in 2008 . . . these green consumers bring enormous clout to the consumer market."[12] If the sleeping dragon ever wakes up, it could be pretty powerful.

Second, there is clearly a feeling in the marketplace that, "if so many well-respected companies are doing this, they must know something we don't." In fact, an argument I've used successfully to convince business leaders to go green is as follows:

"Listen to this list of companies: Starbucks, FedEx-Kinko's, Toyota, Wal-Mart, GE. What is special about these businesses? They're all brand-dominant. When you think coffee, you think Starbucks. When you think mailing a package, you think FedEx, etc. Not only that, they're all incredibly profitable over the long term; they're all extremely well managed; they're all publicly traded and enormously well respected. And you know what? They're all aggressively pursing a green agenda. Something's going on here, and a lot of smart *business*people support it. Might they be on to something?"

A 2006 article in *Brandweek* quoted Judy Hu, global executive director of advertising and branding at General Electric: "Green is green as in the color of money," she said. "It is about a business opportunity, and we believe we can increase our revenue behind these Ecomagination* products and services."[13]

It may be that businesses are not, in fact, convinced that green marketing matters, or that consumers will buy a product because it's green or patronize a store because it's green. But they do care about branding and brand positioning, and they do perceive a trend, or the beginning of a cultural change in our society, even if the evidence for the economic benefits from capitalizing on that trend are slim right now. In a sense, it's not that greenness is becoming more important to the consumer—it's that greenness is becoming part of a normal marketing tableau.

....

*Ecomagination is the brand name for GE green products.

Sustainability Reports: Fluff or Fact?

A key way in which companies market their sustainable business work is through annual sustainability reports. These documents are meant to assess the progress the company has made toward that elusive goal. They are marketing pieces that tout the company's progress and successes, and without exception, they feature pictures of mountains, brooks, and "charismatic megafauna" like elk and deer.

The problem with these reports is that they're sending the wrong message. The reports say, "We're getting 'er done." But in fact, even if a few companies really are getting 'er done (Interface, New Belgium Brewery, and Timberland perhaps), most aren't, even the ones that do care a lot (FedEx, Wal-Mart), because, simply, their carbon footprint is increasing. If these annual reports were presenting the truth, it would be: "We're not making it, dude!"

The bottom line is that this job isn't about the beauty, it's about the mess. It's not about the glory, it's about the dogged pursuit of an enormously challenging goal. This book is testimony to the fact that the sustainable business movement isn't gliding along rails. We're slogging through the mud, struggling with difficult problems that have complex answers. There's contradiction in the very fact of our existence, and uncertainty as to the outcome of our work.

I am constantly asked: "Climate change is big these days. But what's next?" My latest response has been, "Honesty."

The point is that unless we own up to the realities, we'll never be able to get down to solving the real problems. As long as we're buying crap RECs and putting mountain goats on our sustainability reports, we're deluding ourselves. So what should go in the reports? Trash.

In 2006, Aspen Skiing Company's sustainability report had a picture of a "boneyard" on the cover—a pile of scrap metal, empty buckets, old, rusty parts, and other assorted junk. Anyone who has spent time at a ski resort knows what a boneyard is, probably has one himself or herself, and probably isn't too proud of it. The point we were trying to make was that this is about the journey, not the destination. And to some extent, it's about our concept of beauty. The boneyard picture is beautiful because it represents the splendor to be found in the struggle itself.

On the back of the report is a picture of a solar electric system we installed. It too is beautiful, so much so that it has been reprinted in a dozen national magazines. But it's not traditionally beautiful by any definition. It represents the technical solution to a difficult problem. We need to change our concept of beauty as well as our vantage point.

In the mornings several years ago, after checking on the parts washers in Donnie's shop and maybe gazing longingly at the melon launcher, I used to check on the recycle bins outside the vehicle shop to make sure the snowcat drivers hadn't thrown plastic bags in with the bottles and cans, contaminating the recyclables. Sometimes, when I had one hand on the trash bin lid and I was pulling a bag out with the other, I'd find myself pausing, mouth open, to look up at that beautiful Colorado bluebird sky.

It was a sight that confirmed what I always knew: The view from the trenches is the most inspiring. If we can take that vision to the public, with honesty and determination to improve, we can create cadres of loyal customers, maybe even do better as businesses, and make real progress on solving the climate challenge.

The Proximity of
a Sustainable World

> One of the oldest dreams of mankind is to find a
> dignity that might include all living things. And
> one of the greatest of human longings must be to
> bring such dignity to one's own dreams, for each to
> find his or her own life exemplary in some way.
>
> —BARRY LOPEZ. *ARCTIC DREAMS.* 1986

In 2006, Paul Cherrett came from Four Seasons Resort in
Jackson, Wyoming, to take over Aspen Skiing Company's
hospitality programs, including the Little Nell.

Cherrett, who grew up in Florida riding road bikes on the
firm beach sand along the waterline, had a strong environmental ethic. In fact, he explained, he had come to Aspen
Skiing Company because of its corporate culture and values,
including its environmental commitments. At the Four Seasons, he had implemented the "Eco Luxe," a package that
enabled guests to choose a room tricked out with environmentally friendly features and that donated a portion of the

room fee to a local environmental organization. He also got rid of the bottled water and replaced it with a crystal pitcher of fresh, local tap water; by eliminating 52,000 Evian bottles annually, he saved the company $37,000.

Within the first few weeks in Aspen, Cherrett came into my office to ask about taking the bus.

"Heck," he said, "I used to ride the bus when I was in Vancouver and Seattle. I loved it."

In fact, riding the bus from Basalt, where Paul lived, to our offices is easy and relaxing. Instead of driving and having to pay attention to avoid rear-ending the car in front of you, you can sit back and read the local papers. And riding the bus saves money, too, because Aspen Skiing Company subsidizes the cost of a bus pass.

The next Monday Cherrett showed up in my office looking quite strained and agitated. He told me about his bus experience.

He had arrived at the stop, a short walk from his house, fairly easily. But when the bus came, it was packed. Paul wears the same kind of fancy clothes Eric Calderon at the Nell used to wear—pressed shirts, nice slacks. And it was hot on the bus—extremely hot. Instead of reading the papers, Paul had to stand, sweating. As he rapidly pitted out his pressed shirt, he said, "people were looking at me like, 'Who's the idiot? Dressed like that, can't he afford a car? And why is he sweating so much? Is there something wrong with him?'"

Unfamiliar with local bus procedures, Paul didn't know that when the bus driver announced, "Airport" (where our offices are), you had to pull the cord if you wanted the bus to stop. Paul missed the stop as a result and had to get off at the next stop, Buttermilk Mountain. Then, instead of walking back on the bike path (which he didn't know about), he waited half an hour for the next bus going in the opposite direction.

Finally arriving at work an hour late, soaking with sweat and needing a change of clothes, Paul wasn't particularly happy. But it got worse. At 5:20, when it was time to catch the bus home, it was *hailing* outside. Paul came to my office in despair. I told him we'd take the later bus, and I'd escort him. When we arrived at the bus stop, there were three toothless homeless men there, drinking beer from cans in paper bags. They apparently weren't waiting for the bus, just using the kiosk as a shelter to drink in. Paul asked, "Is there one for me?"

When the bus arrived, Paul was so stunned that he simply handed the bus driver his pass. After an awkward, silent pause, the driver said, "Uh . . . where are you going?"

"Oh, sorry. Basalt." Some bus riders laughed, as if to say, *How could anyone be so clueless?*

Paul's story is partly about being the new guy in town. And as a vice president in charge of a five-star hotel in Aspen, his story doesn't garner sympathy. ("The poor executive had to ride *the bus*! And he got *wet*!") But it's also about how difficult it is to do the right thing, the green thing, or the climate-saving thing, even on the most irrelevant and microcosmic level. Doing so represents a departure from business as usual, and that inevitably means hassles, costs, and anxiety. And yet we need to do this on a global scale.

Given the extreme obstacles we'll always face in dealing with climate change, it's worth asking the question: What will motivate us to keep going forward and actually pull this off? How will we become—and then remain—inspired for the long slog ahead? Because this battle will take not just political will and corporate action—it will also require an unyielding commitment and dedication on the part of all humanity. *We need to remake society.* Is it possible for us to find motivators strong enough to make this extended climate struggle successful and to help us sustain it over the years?

We can intellectualize the need for action all we want, as I did in Chapter 2. But in the end, I've found, our motivation usually comes down to a cliché: our kids and, for want of a better word, our dignity.

Walter Bennett, Chainsaw Redneck

People often ask to meet with me to talk about climate, sustainable business, and the environment. One day I got a call from a guy named Walter Bennett. Walter worked for Stihl (pronounced "steel"), the German chainsaw manufacturer. Aspen Skiing Company has a partnership with Stihl, which sponsors free-skiing competitions, and we use Stihl saws on our mountains to cut trails. (One new trail is called "Stihletto" in honor of the company.) Like a John Deere hat, a Stihl hat—particularly a foam-backed trucker cap—says you're an authentic, blue-collar grunt. Ski patrol loves them.

Walter wanted to meet to talk about climate change, and I agreed, though I didn't expect much from the meeting. This was, after all, a guy from a chainsaw manufacturer.

When he walked in the room, my hopes of a progressive discussion dropped even further. In his midfifties, with a crew cut and graying hair, Walter looked like, and described himself as, a West Texas redneck. He was the epitome of the gray-haired Cheney-esque board members I've been hoping will die off so we can actually start doing something on climate. He announced that he had just had a grandchild: his daughter had given birth to a baby boy. He pulled out his laptop and hooked it up to his projector.

"Do you mind if I show you this presentation I've prepared for my senior management?"

"No problem," I said, thinking, *Get me out of here.*

Walter clicked a button and blew my mind. He had prepared an hour-long multimedia event on climate change, complete with country music overlays, video clips, and charts and graphs that rivaled any presentation I've seen from experts in the field, nonprofit heads, Al Gore, and climate PhDs. It got the science, the challenges, and some of the solutions exactly right. Walter's goal was to convince Stihl that it should begin to take action on climate change, in concert with its efforts to develop cleaner-burning chainsaws and other power tools.

When Walter was done, I sat in stunned silence. It was a while before I could muster any sort of response. When I could speak, I asked:

"Walter, if you don't mind my asking . . . what was it that moved a Texas redneck like you to care about climate change at all, let alone try to change an entire corporation's perspective on the issue? You don't really fit the mold of someone who would do this."

Walter said: "Holding my grandchild—holding that little baby in my hands. . . . " His voice trailed off. I thought he was going to cry. I thought *I* was going to cry.

Walter's visceral realization of the implications of climate change is spreading, I believe, throughout the country and throughout the world. It is occurring because climate change is a threat the likes of which our society has never seen. Unlike predictions of doom from environmentalists early in the century (the population bomb, for example), this one has uniform scientific support. It is happening, and it will get worse.

The journalist Bill Moyers related a similar experience when he accepted Harvard Medical School's Global Environment Citizen Award in 2004. He described reading the news—about reports coming out from policy groups funded by ExxonMobil that claimed climate change is a myth; about congressional bills that included riders to remove all endangered species protections from pesticides; and about other insults to the environment. Looking up from his desk, Moyers saw the pictures of his grandchildren on his desk:

I see the future looking back at me from those photographs. . . . We are . . . betraying their trust. Despoiling their world. . . . On the heath Lear asks Gloucester: "How do you see the world?" And Gloucester, who is blind, answers: "I see it feelingly."

I see it feelingly.

. . .The will to fight is the antidote to despair . . . and the answer to those faces looking back at me from those photographs on my desk. What we need to match the science of human health is what the ancient Israelites called "hocma"—the science of the heart . . . the capacity to see . . . to feel . . . and then to act . . . as if the future depended on you. Believe me, it does.

Moyers, an ordained Baptist minister, taps into something positively religious about the possibilities in a grand movement to protect the earth. Climate change offers us something immensely valuable and difficult to find in the modern world: the opportunity to participate in a movement that—in its vastness of scope—can fulfill the human need for a sense of meaning in our lives.

Recently, I received an e-mail from Bob Janes, an Alaskan tour guide I met in 2007. He wrote:

My interests are being drawn more and more towards the global warming issue (whose aren't?). I am able to involve myself (both personally and in a business capacity) now and into the future, but am definitely in the dark on a specific course. . . .

Do you believe one can actually find a way to earn a bit of a living in this emerging (crisis?), and at the same time go home at night and let the kids know that something good is being accomplished? My business sense tells me there are many grand opportunities, but the field seems to be a tempting invitation to intrusive species and interests. What is reality? What will stand the test of time?

When I tried to pinpoint what Bob was talking about and find an answer to his question, I ended up with words that didn't square with my scientific background or the empirical perspective that the field of sustainability and climate has historically taken. The words I found to describe Bob's goals came from the religious community—words like "grace," "dignity," "redemption," and "compassion." And it occurred to me that the environmental and political world, in its discussion of climate change and its solutions, has been missing something fundamental.

Scores of books have been published on climate change and sustainable business over the last two decades. Most come from secular academics in the left-leaning environmental community or free market–crazed economists at right-wing think tanks. They offer either pure science or pure economics.

Few to none of these books address the broader, seemingly glaring point that no such holistically encompassing opportunity as solving climate change, nothing with so great a promise to achieve some universal human goals, on so large a scale, has been offered up since the establishment of large organized religions between two and four thousand years ago. Even the growing evangelical climate movement focuses on a biblical mandate for stewardship more than on the human search for meaning. But the vision of a sustainable society, with its implications for equity, social justice, happiness, and hope, embodies the primary aspirations of most religious traditions: finding a way to live at peace with each other, the world, and our consciences; achieving a graceful existence; and building a framework for a noble life. Most religions have evolved to meet the basic human need for community, understanding, and mission. Religion, in this original intent, and the sustainability movement seem to be sourced from the same ancient human wellspring.

This is a hopeful concept: Maybe humans are hardwired to engage in, and relish, a challenge like the problem of solving climate change.

In 1927, when Charles Lindbergh completed his solo flight across the Atlantic, F. Scott Fitzgerald wrote: "Something bright and alien flashed across the sky . . . and for a moment people set down their glasses in country clubs and speakeasies and thought of their old best dreams." Perhaps solving climate change fulfills one of our oldest dreams. And maybe something even better: maybe we can't help but do it. The very nature of human longing suggests that we simply can't turn down this opportunity to imbue our lives with meaning, dignity, hope, vision, and grace. Solving climate change is in our blood and bones.

Most important, we've done it before. My Grandpa Joe, who was born in 1901 in Fargo, North Dakota, and died in 1997, lived part of his long life in a time of horses and carriages, woodstoves, local food, limited pollution, and almost entirely renewable energy. Most of our grandparents lived in a sustainable world. In our darkest moments, we have the memory of them as a touchstone: *I have touched a person who lived in a sustainable society. I sat on his lap, I kissed him good-night. I have his wristwatch in my dresser drawer.*

What we need to do is that close, that real, that personal, that tangible, that possible.

You are not expected to complete the task.
Neither are you allowed to put it down.

—THE TALMUD

CHAPTER 1: TRENCH WARFARE, NOT SURGERY

1. Rosenthal, 2007.
2. Romm, 2008.
3. Eilperin, 2008.
4. Malin and Boehland, 2002, p. 11.
5. Visit the Purl Wax Web site at: http://purlracing.com/osc/catalog/privacy.php.
6. Crook, 2008, p. 32.
7. Bailey, 2007, p. 3.

CHAPTER 2: CLIMATE CHANGE AND THE FIERCE URGENCY OF NOW

1. United Nations, World Commission on Environment and Development, 1987, p. 8.
2. Vaitheeswaran, 2003, p. 3.
3. Hansen, 2008.
4. Quoted in Pearson, 2006, p. 93.
5. Kolbert, *Field Notes*, 2006, p. 189.
6. Romm, 2007, p. 63.
7. Gertner, 2006, p. 41.
8. Flannery, 2005, p. 254.

9. Zweibel, Mason, and Fthenakis, 2007.

10. Personal conversation, spring 2006.

11. Braiker, 2006.

12. Bukowski, 2000.

CHAPTER 3: SUSTAINABILITY, FORK-SPLIT

1. Stipp, 2002.

CHAPTER 4: ASPEN

1. Larson, 2003.

2. Shellenberger and Nordhaus, 2004.

3. Foreman, 2005.

4. Lipsher and Human, 2005.

5. See "Western Colorado's Climate Data" at the Canary Initiative Web site: http://www.aspenglobalwarming.com/western coloradodata.cfm. Climate science writer Susan Hassol came up with the great click-and-drag analogy.

6. Aspen Global Change Institute, 2006.

7. Colorado College, 2006, p. 97.

8. University of California at Davis, 2007.

9. Healy, 2007.

10. The latest is University of Maryland, 2008.

11. Saunders, Montgomery, and Easley, 2008, p. iv.

12. Calculations courtesy of Randy Udall.

13. Friedman, 2008.

14. Comment by alpha6 on Conniff, 2007.

CHAPTER 5: FINDING YOUR BIGGEST LEVER

1. Fishman, 2006.

2. Rosenberg, 2006.

3. Kolbert, "Untransformed," 2006.

4. McKibben, 2007.

5. Nordhaus and Shellenberger, 2007.

6. Romm, "The Death of 'The Death of Environmentalism,'" 2007.

7. Royal Dutch/Shell, 2001, p. 22.

8. Hansen, 2006.

9. Marolt, 2007.

CHAPTER 6: SUSTAINABLE SUSTAINABILITY

1. Gunther, 2007.

2. T. J. Rodgers, letter to Jim Wright, president of Dartmouth College, July 21, 2006 (shared with me by Rodgers).

3. Ibid.

4. Portions of this section originally appeared in the *Journal of Industrial Ecology* under the title "Priming the Pump for Emissions Reduction," October 2006, pp. 8–10.

CHAPTER 7: GREEN ENERGY

1. Energy Information Administration, 2008.

2. For a quick summary, see Environmental Defense Fund, 2007.

3. McKinsey Global Institute, 2007, p. 9.

4. Auffhammer and Carson, 2008.

5. Bradsher and Barboza, 2006.

6. Stoner, 2006.

7. Available at: http://makower.typepad.com/joel_makower/2006/12/are_carbon_offs.html.

8. Mark Trexler, e-mail exchange, November 2006.

9. Climate Group, 2008.

10. United Nations, 2008.

CHAPTER 8: GREEN BUILDINGS

1. Statistics available at: http://www.usgbc.org/ShowFile.aspx?DocumentID=3340 and http://www.usgbc.org/DisplayPage.aspx?CMSPageID=1718. The blimp calculation is based on average

household emissions of 26,000 pounds, estimated in Heede, 2002. The Goodyear blimp's volume is 202,000 cubic feet, equivalent to about 23,000 pounds of CO_2.

2. Mazria, 2003.

3. Some of the material in this chapter comes from Schendler and Udall, 2005, a paper I wrote with Randy Udall. My thanks to Randy for permission to use this material.

4. Stein and Reiss, 2004.

5. Frangos, 2005.

6. Lipsher, 2008.

7. Roberts, 2007.

8. Winston Churchill, speech at the Harrow School, October 29, 1941.

9. Wilson, 2007.

10. Holdren, 2008.

CHAPTER 9: SHAMELESS SELF-PROMOTION AND WHY IT MATTERS

1. Lewis, 1995.

2. Mooney, 2005.

3. Karliner, 1997, p. 171.

4. O'Carrol, 2008.

5. Bruno, 2000.

6. The campaign can be found at: http://www.chevrolet.com/fuelsolutions/.

7. Reuters, 2008.

8. Fowler, 2002.

9. Murphy, 2003.

10. Landor and Associates, 2006.

11. An extensive discussion of the proprietary study is available at: http://makower.typepad.com/joel_makower/2007/07/green-consumers.html, and also at www.yankelovich.com.

12. Simmons Research, 2007.

13. Melilio and Miller, 2006.

BIBLIOGRAPHY

Anderson, Ray C. *Mid-Course Correction: Toward a Sustainable Enterprise: The Interface Model.* Atlanta: Peregrinzilla Press, 1998.

Aspen Global Change Institute. "Climate Change and Aspen: An Assessment of Potential Impacts and Responses." 2006. Available at: http://www.agci.org/aspenStudy.html.

Auffhammer, Maximilian, and Richard T. Carson. "Forecasting the Path of China's CO_2 Emissions Using Province-Level Information." *Journal of Environmental Impacts and Management* 55, no. 3, May 2008, pp. 229–247.

Bailey, John. "Lessons from the Pioneers: Tackling Global Warming at the Local Level." Institute for Local Self-Reliance (ILSR), January 2007. Available at: http://www.newrules.org/de/pioneers.pdf.

Bradsher, Keith, and David Barboza. "Pollution from Chinese Coal Casts a Global Shadow." *New York Times*, June 11, 2006.

Brown, Lester. *Plan B 3.0: Mobilizing to Save Civilization.* New York: Norton, 2008.

Bruno, Kenny. "Shell: Clouding the Issue." Corpwatch, November 15, 2000. Available at: http://www.corpwatch.org/article.php?id=218.

Bukowski, Charles. *What Matters Most Is How Well You Walk Through the Fire.* Boston: Black Sparrow Press, 2000.

Casey, Susan. "Patagonia: Blueprint for Green Business: The Story of How Patagonia Founder Yvon Chouinard Took His Passion for the Outdoors and Turned It into an Amazing Business." *Fortune*, May 29, 2007.

Chouinard, Yvon. "Patagonia: The Next 100 Years." In *Sacred Trusts: Essays on Stewardship and Responsibility*, ed. Michael Katakis. San Francisco: Mercury House, 1993.

———. *Let My People Go Surfing: The Education of a Reluctant Businessman.* New York: Penguin, 2005.

Clean Air–Cool Planet. "A Consumer's Guide to Retail Carbon Offset Providers." December 2006. Available at: http://www .cleanair-coolplanet.org/ConsumersGuidetoCarbonOffsets .pdf.

Climate Group. "China's Clean Revolution." August 2008. Available at: http://www.theclimategroup.org/assets/resources/ Chinas_Clean_Revolution.pdf.

Colorado College. "The 2006 Colorado College State of the Rockies Report Card." Available at: http://www.colorado college.edu/StateoftheRockies/06ReportCard.html.

Conniff, Michael. "Con Games: Canary Dead on Arrival in Aspen." *Aspen Post,* February 8, 2007. Available at: http:// www.aspenpost.net/2007/02/08/con-games-canary-dead-on -arrival-in-aspen/.

Crook, Clive. "Sins of Emission." *Atlantic Monthly,* April 2008, pp. 32–34.

Diamond, Jared. *Collapse: How Societies Choose to Fail or Succeed.* New York: Viking, 2005.

Eilperin, Juliet. "Severe Weather to Increase as Earth Warms." *Washington Post,* June, 19, 2008.

Elgin, Ben. "Little Green Lies: The Bitter Education of a Corporate Environmentalist." *Business Week,* October 29, 2007. Available at: http://www.businessweek.com/magazine/con tent/07_44/b4056001.htm.

Energy Information Administration. "Annual Energy Outlook 2008." June 2008. Available at: www.eia.doe.gov/oiaf/aeo/.

Environmental Defense Fund. "The Cap and Trade Success Story." Posted February 12, 2007; updated September 17, 2007. Available at: http://www.edf.org/page.cfm?tagID=1085.

Esty, Daniel, and Andrew Winston. *Green to Gold: How Smart Companies Use Environmental Strategy to Innovate, Create Value, and Build Competitive Advantage.* New Haven, Conn.: Yale University Press, 2006.

Fickett, Arnold, Clark Gellings, and Amory Lovins. "Efficient Use of Electricity." *Scientific American*, September 1990.

Fishman, Charles. "How Many Lightbulbs Does It Take to Change the World? One. And You're Looking at It." *Fast Company*, September 2006. Available at: http://www.fast company.com/magazine/108/open_lightbulbs.html.

Flannery, Tim. *The Weather Makers: How Man Is Changing the Climate and What It Means for Life on Earth*. New York: Atlantic Monthly Press, 2005.

Foreman, Dave. "Nature's Crisis." *Counterpunch*, March 26, 2005. Available at: http://www.counterpunch.org/foreman0326 2005.html.

Fowler, G. A. "'Green' Sales Pitch Isn't Moving Many Products." *Wall Street Journal*, March 6, 2002.

Frangos, Alex. "Is It Too Easy Being Green? Eco-Friendly Certification Is Big with Builders, Tenants; Critics See a 'Broken' System." *Wall Street Journal*, October 19, 2005.

Frey, Darcy. "Watching the World Melt Away: The Future as Seen by a Lonely Scientist at the End of the Earth." *New York Times Magazine*, January 6, 2002.

Friedman, Benjamin M. *The Moral Consequences of Economic Growth*. New York: Vintage, 2008.

Friedman, Thomas L. *The Lexus and the Olive Tree: Understanding Globalization*. New York: Farrar, Straus & Giroux, 1999.

_____. *Hot, Flat, and Crowded: Why We Need a Green Revolution—and How It Can Renew America*. New York: Farrar, Straus & Giroux, 2008.

Gelbspan, Ross. *Boiling Point: How Politicians, Big Oil and Coal, Journalists, and Activists Have Fueled the Climate Crisis—And What We Can Do to Avert Disaster*. New York: Basic Books, 2004.

Gertner, Jon. "The Nuclear Option." *New York Times Magazine*, July 16, 2006, pp. 36–64.

Goodell, Jeff. "How Coal Got Its Glow Back." *New York Times Magazine*, July 22, 2001.

Gore, Al. *Earth in the Balance: Ecology and the Human Spirit.* Boston: Houghton Mifflin, 1992.

_____. *An Inconvenient Truth.* Emmaus, Penn.: Rodale, 2006.

_____. *The Assault on Reason.* New York: Penguin Press, 2007.

Gunther, Marc. "The Future's So Bright, I Gotta Wear Shades." *Fortune,* October 15, 2007.

Hansen, James. "The Threat to the Planet." *New York Review of Books,* July 13, 2006. Available at: http://www.nybooks.com/articles/19131.

_____. 2008. "Tipping Point: Perspective of a Climatologist." *State of the Wild* (Wildlife Conservation Society). Available at: http://www.columbia.edu/~jeh1/2008/State-OfWild_20080428.pdf.

Harvard Business Review. *Harvard Business Review on Business and the Environment.* Boston: Harvard Business School Press, 2000.

_____. *Harvard Business Review on Green Business Strategy.* Boston: Harvard Business School Press, 2007.

Hawken, Paul. *The Ecology of Commerce: A Declaration of Sustainability.* New York: HarperCollins, 1993.

_____. *Blessed Unrest: How the Largest Movement in the World Came into Being and Why No One Saw It Coming.* New York: Viking, 2007.

Hawken, Paul, Amory Lovins, and L. Hunter Lovins. *Natural Capitalism: Creating the Next Industrial Revolution.* Boston: Little, Brown, 1999.

Healy, Rita. "Aspen vs. Vail: The War Turns Green." *Time,* August 6, 2007. Available at: http://www.time.com/time/business/article/0,8599,1650342,00.html.

Heede, Richard. "Cool Citizens: Everyday Solutions to Climate Change." Rocky Mountain Institute, April 9, 2002. Available at: http://www.rmi.org/sitepages/pid173.php.

Holdren, John. "One Last Chance to Lead." *Scientific American Earth 3.0.* September 2008.

Karliner, Joshua. *The Corporate Planet: Ecology and Politics in the Age of Globalization.* San Francisco: Sierra Club Books, 1997.

Kennedy, Robert F., Jr. *Crimes Against Nature: How George W. Bush and His Corporate Pals Are Plundering the Country and Hijacking Our Democracy.* New York: HarperCollins, 2004.

Kidder, Tracy. *Mountains Beyond Mountains: The Quest of Dr. Paul Farmer, a Man Who Would Cure the World.* New York: Random House, 2003.

Kolbert, Elizabeth. *Field Notes from a Catastrophe: Man, Nature, and Climate Change.* New York: Bloomsbury, 2006. Originally published as "The Climate of Man," *New Yorker*, May 9, 2005.

———. "Untransformed." *New Yorker*, September 25, 2006. Available at: http://www.newyorker.com/archive/2006/09/25/060925ta_talk_kolbert.

Landor and Associates. "New Study by Landor Associates Reveals Most Consumers Don't Care About 'Green.'" July 6, 2006. Available at: http://www.landor.com/index.cfm?do=news.pressrelease&storyid=464&bhcp=1.

Larson, Erik. *The Devil in the White City: Murder, Magic, and Madness at the Fair That Changed America.* New York: Crown, 2003.

Lewis, Paul. "Rights Group Says Shell Oil Shares Blame." *New York Times*, November 11, 1995. Available at: http://query.nytimes.com/gst/fullpage.html?res=9B0CE6D81439F932A25752C1A963958260#.

Lipsher, Steve. "Aspen Vacation Homes: Energy Hogs Sprawling, Little-Used Second Homes Sock It to Aspen by Generating Most of Its Residential Greenhouse Gases." *Denver Post*, August 30, 2008.

Lopez, Barry. *Arctic Dreams: Imagination and Desire in a Northern Landscape.* New York: Scribner's, 1986.

Malin, Nadav, and Jessica Boehland. "Oberlin College's Lewis Center." *Environmental Building News*, July-August 2002, p. 11.

Marolt, Roger. "Save the Planet, Eat a Booger." *Aspen Times*, March 16, 2007. Available at: http://www.aspentimes.com/ article/20070316/COLUMN/103160049&parentprofile =search.

Mazria, Edward. "It's the Architecture, Stupid!" *Solar Today*, May-June 2003, pp. 48–51. Available at: http://www.mazria.com/ ItsTheArchitectureStupid.pdf.

McDonough, William, and Michael Braungart. *Cradle to Cradle: Remaking the Way We Make Things*. New York: North Point Press, 2002.

McKibben, Bill. *The End of Nature*. New York: Random House, 1989.

_____. "The Unsung Solution." *Orion*, November-December 2007.

_____. *The Bill McKibben Reader*. New York: Holt, 2008.

McKinsey Global Institute. "Curbing Global Energy Demand Growth: The Energy Productivity Opportunity" (executive summary). May 2007. Available (with registration) at: http://mckinsey.com/mgi/reports/pdfs/Curbing_Global _Energy/Curbing_Global_Energy_executive_summary.pdf.

Melilio, Wendy, and Steve Miller. "Companies Find It's Not Easy Marketing Green: A Glut of Eco-Friendly Campaigns Have Consumers Feeling Jaded and Confused." *Brandweek*, July 24, 2006.

Mendelsohn, Robert, and James E. Neumann, eds. *The Impact of Climate Change on the United States Economy*. Cambridge, U.K.: Cambridge University Press, 1999.

Mooney, Chris. "As the World Burns." *Mother Jones*, May-June 2005.

Murphy, Cait. "The Next Big Thing: Move Aside, Tree Huggers. More and More Hardheaded Entrepreneurs Are Tapping into the Growing Green Movement." *Fortune Small Business*, June 1, 2003.

Nordhaus, Ted, and Michael Shellenberger. "Second Life: A Manifesto for a New Environmentalism." *New Republic*, September 24, 2007, pp. 30–33.

O'Carrol, Eoin. "Exxon-Mobil Cuts Off (Some) Funding to Climate Deniers." *Christian Science Monitor*, May 29, 2008. Available at: http://features.csmonitor.com/environment/ 2008/05/29/exxonmobil-cuts-off-funding-to-some-climate -deniers/.

Pearson, Stephanie. "Eco All-Stars: Heidi Cullen." *Outside*, March 2006.

Reuters. "GM Exec Stands by Calling Global Warming 'a Crock.'" Reuters, February 22, 2008. Available at: http://www.reuters .com/article/latestCrisis/idUSN22372976.

Roberts, David. "A Public Policy Gimme: Financing Green Construction and Retrofits." *Huffington Post*, December 17, 2007. Available at: http://www.huffingtonpost.com/david-roberts/a-public-policy-gimme-fi_b_77188.html.

Romm, Joseph J. *Lean and Clean Management: How to Boost Profits and Productivity by Reducing Pollution*. New York: Kodansha, 1994.

_____. *Cool Companies: How the Best Businesses Boost Profits and Productivity by Cutting Greenhouse Gas Emissions*. Washington, DC: Island Press, 1999.

_____. *Hell and High Water: Global Warming—the Solution and the Politics—and What We Should Do*. New York: Morrow, 2007.

_____. "The Cold Truth About Climate Change." *Salon.com*, February 27, 2008. Available at: http://salon.com/news /feature/2008/02/27/global_warming_deniers/print.html.

Rosenthal, Elizabeth. "UN Chief Seeks More Climate Change Leadership." *New York Times*, November 18, 2007.

Royal Dutch/Shell. "Energy Needs, Choices, and Responsibilities: Scenarios to 2050" (2001 report). Available at: http://www .cleanenergystates.org/CaseStudies/Shell_2050.pdf.

Saunders, Stephen, and Maureen Maxwell. *Less Snow, Less Water: Climate Disruption in the West*. Rocky Mountain Climate Organization, September 2005.

Saunders, Stephen, Charles Montgomery, and Tom Easley. *Hotter and Drier: The West's Changed Climate*. Rocky Mountain Climate Organization, March 2008.

Schendler, Auden, and Randy Udall. "LEED Is Broken . . . Let's Fix It." 2005. Available at: http://www.aspensnowmass.com/ environment/images/LEEDisBroken.pdf.

Scientific American. "Energy's Future Beyond Carbon: How to Power the Economy and Still Fight Global Warming." *Scientific American* special issue, September 2006.

Shellenberger, Michael, and Ted Nordhaus. "The Death of Environmentalism: Global Warming Politics in a Post-Environmental World." 2004. Available at: http://www.thebreakthrough.org/ images/Death_of_Environmentalism.pdf.

Simmons Research. "Sow Your Targeting Seeds with Green Consumers." Marketing & Research Data Consultants (MRDC), November 6, 2007. Available at: http://www.market researchworld.net/index.php?option=content&task=view&id =1681&Itemid=.

Singer, Peter. *How Are We to Live? Ethics in an Age of Self-Interest.* New York: Prometheus Books, 1993.

Speth, James Gustave. *Red Sky at Morning: America and the Crisis of the Global Environment.* New Haven, Conn.: Yale University Press, 2004.

_____. *The Bridge at the Edge of the World: Capitalism, the Environment, and Crossing from Crisis to Sustainability.* New Haven, Conn.: Yale University Press, 2008.

Stein, Jay, and Rachel Reiss. 2004. "Ensuring the Sustainability of Sustainable Design: What Designers Need to Know About LEED." Esource, paper AED-04–01. Available at: http:// greenbuildings.platts.com.

Stoner, Edward. "Vail Resorts Goes 100 Percent Wind Power . . . Becomes Second-Largest Corporate Buyer of Wind Power in the U.S." *Vail Daily*, August 1, 2006.

Stratus Consulting. "Climate Change in Park City: Executive Summary." January 5, 2007. Available at: http://www .parkcitymountain.com/sos/Executive_Summary.pdf.

Swisher, Joel N. *The New Business Climate: A Guide to Lower Carbon Emissions and Better Business Performance.* Snowmass, Colo.: Rocky Mountain Institute, 2002.

United Nations Environment Program. "Global Trends in Sustainable Energy Investment 2008: Analysis of Trends and Issues in the Financing of Renewable Energy and Energy Efficiency." Available at: http://sefi.unep.org/fileadmin/media/sefi/docs/publications/Global_Trends_2008.pdf.

United Nations World Commission on Environment and Development. *Our Common Future.* New York: Oxford University Press, 1987.

University of California at Davis, Tahoe Environmental Research Center. "Tahoe State of the Lake Report." 2007. Available at: http://terc.ucdavis.edu/stateofthelake/StateOfThe-Lake2007.pdf.

University of Maryland, Center for Integrative Environmental Research. "Economic Impacts of Climate Change on Colorado: A Review and Assessment." July 2008. Available at: http://www.cier.umd.edu/climateadaptation/Colorado%20Economic%20Impacts%20of%20Climate%20Change.pdf.

U.S. Global Change Research Program, National Assessment Synthesis Team. *Climate Change Impacts on the United States: The Potential Consequences of Climate Variability and Change.* Cambridge, U.K.: Cambridge University Press, 2000.

Vaitheeswaran, Vijay V. *Power to the People: How the Coming Energy Revolution Will Transform an Industry, Change Our Lives, and Maybe Even Save the Planet.* New York: Farrar, Straus & Giroux, 2003.

Wilson, Alex. "An Environmental Service Corps for America." *Environmental Building News,* July 1, 2007. Available at: http://www.buildinggreen.com/auth/article.cfm/2007/7/10/An-Environmental-Service-Corps-for-America/.

Wilson, Alex, et al. *Green Development: Integrating Ecology and Real Estate.* New York: Wiley, 1998.

Zweibel, Ken, James Mason, and Vasilis Fthenakis. "A Solar Grand Plan: By 2050 Solar Power Could End U.S. Dependence on Foreign Oil and Slash Greenhouse Gas Emissions." *Scientific American,* January 2007.

CREDITS

Quotes from Joe Romm's book *Hell and High Water: Global Warming—the Solution and the Politics—and What We Should Do* and his blog www.climateprogress.org are reprinted with Romm's permission.

Randy Udall is quoted with his permission. Thanks also to Randy Udall for permission to use a section of our paper "LEED Is Broken . . . Let's Fix It."

Thanks to Ed Marston for permission to use the discussion of Aspen as a world's fair in progress, which came from an article we cowrote.

ACKNOWLEDGMENTS

This book evolved from my experiences at Aspen Skiing Company. Our work there was characterized by a unique freedom—to speak and act and push the envelope in ways that were sometimes awkward but always in the service of a greater cause—driving change on crucial environmental issues. The freedom I experienced there—which was, simply, unmatched elsewhere in the corporate world—was initially conceived and militantly backed by former CEO Pat O'Donnell; unwaveringly supported by my longtime boss David Bellack; built upon and expanded by current CEO Mike Kaplan; and anchored by managing partner Jim Crown. I owe these people—who are not just bosses but friends—a debt I can't repay. To quote Yvon Chouinard, they gave me the freedom to pursue my chosen craft.

It was the employees of Aspen Skiing Company, past and present, who made this book possible. This is their story, not mine, and I have been privileged to spend a decade among this universally fine group of people.

The Crown family consistently supported our work, talked with me about it, opened doors for me to engage on a broader level, and worked to make their own lives part of our shared vision. In particular these supporters include Lester, Jim, Susan, Steve, and Paula Crown and Bill Kunkler.

My old friend and companion in outdoor adventure, Randy Udall, has been a profound influence on my thinking. (To the extent that I've gotten into trouble over the years, I'd suggest that it's his fault.) He is quoted extensively in this book because he's as clear a thinker on the subject of climate as anyone I know. That he spends any time on energy and climate work given how much he'd rather be outside skiing or hiking is testimony to the fact that, to paraphrase Stanley Kunitz, he "loves the earth so much." His wife Leslie and their amazing children, Ren, Tarn, and Torrey, have been a welcome presence in my family's life.

My uncle Roger Smith and his brother Ted took me into the Bob Marshall Wilderness when I was fourteen on a grueling and punishing twenty-four-mile hike with obsolete packs, nonfunctional sleeping bags, and no ground pads, and for that I'm eternally grateful. Ted, who ran and was responsible for the relentless innovation at the Kendall Foundation for many years, has been a friend, mentor, and influence my whole life, from driving me to visit colleges to advising me on careers and tennis rackets.

This book would not have existed without backup from the virtuoso journalist and best-selling author Charles Fishman at *Fast Company* magazine, who has been almost pathologically selfless in support of me, providing endless time and advice. When I asked him, "How do you write a book?" Fish led me down the road from day one. He is a good and gracious man.

When I interned at *High Country News* almost twenty years ago, Ed and Betsy Marston became my friends, and they have been teaching me how to write ever since. I would be a different, lesser person without that experience, their teaching, and our friendship. Florence Williams, who was also at HCN, remains a key friend and writing adviser.

Dr. Joseph Romm, whom I quote extensively in this book, is the smartest and most level-headed thinker on climate and energy policy and action I know. He, too, has been enormously generous with his time and work. Visit www.climateprogress.org for the best climate blog going.

Amory and Hunter Lovins hired me at Rocky Mountain Institute and have supported me ever since. This book relies heavily on Amory's ideas, and anything I've done is grounded in his vision and work. I'm proud to know Amory and Hunter and to have worked as closely as I did with both of them. At Rocky Mountain Institute, I also had the privilege of working with Paul Hawken, whose seminal writing informs every piece of my work.

Tom Friedman at the *New York Times* has been generous with his ideas and his ear and is always willing to talk about book writing, climate, and energy. Barry Lopez's writing made a profound impact on me when I was twelve and has guided me ever since. I thank him for generously sharing his writing and for his words of encouragement. The writing and activism of Bill McKibben, Robert Kennedy Jr., Al Gore, Yvon Chouinard, James Hansen, and Gus Speth have been vitally important and influential. David Brower left an indelible impression on me when I had the privilege of meeting him. My in-laws, Fran and Sanford Freedman, with their ebullient support and interest, helped me get through the book-writing process. Others who have influenced and encouraged me over the years include Topher Smith, Lib Smith, and Rachel Schendler; Cador Jones (who was my coworker during the trailer-insulating days), Drew Jones, and Peter Mueller, my stock companions on many life adventures, most of them in remote locations, mental and physical; Chris Lotspeich and Ross Jacobs; Penn Newhard, Jack Aley, Walter Bennett, Bob Janes, Liz and Tom Penzel, Stu and Shelley Uffrig, John Katzenberger, Tom Golec, and Thierry Burkhart; Matt Hamilton, who works with me at Aspen Skiing Company and is a sane and invaluable sounding board; Stephen Kanipe, Dan Bakal, Vijay Vaitheeswaran, Don Chen, Adam Werbach, Robert and Marcie Musser, Joe Lstiburek, Betsy Petit, Mike Brylawski, Greg Williams, Mike Gibbs, Rob Russell, Jen and Dave Cramer, John Steelman, Theo Spencer, Stephen Saunders, Jim Kravitz, Tom Cardamone, Tom Udall, Brad Udall, Jon Fox-Rubin, Rocky Anderson, Rick Heede, John Gitchell, Dave Houghton, August Hasz, Matt Jay, Jamie Rooney, Scott Munro, Terry Kellogg, Michael Hassig, Michael Kinsley at RMI, and Norbert Klebl; ex-interns and now superstar greenies in their own right, Mike Lichtenfeld and Greg Stiles; John McBride and Piper Foster at the Sopris Foundation; Joel Makower, Dr. Mark Trexler, Dan Richardson, Joani Matranga, and Adam Palmer; all the eco-partners, past and present, have been good friends and valuable resources, including Derek Smith, Ben Packard, Sean Schmidt,

David Binnell, Denise Taschereau, Jill Zilligan, Larry Rogero, Jill Dumain, Nancy Hirshberg, Andrea Asche, Eric Willmans, Eric Brody, Bruce Schlein, Betsy Blaisdell, Reed Doyle, and Dave Reed. Dr. Mike Brown remains a valuable friend and supportive "elder" in this field who is always there for advice, surf lessons, and/or a beer(s). At ASC, now or in the past, and in addition to those I've already mentioned, I'm grateful to Matt Jones, my friend who is defining what it means to be a CFO in the age of climate change; John Rigney and his team, who with great humor and cutting sarcasm have pushed ASC's agenda out into other businesses and events; Sue Lucks, Rob Covington, Frank White, Jan Koorn, Rich Burkley, Bill Kane, David Corbin, and Jim Laing; Derek Johnson, Anne Cerrone, Chris Kiley, John Norton, Gert Van Moorsel, Victor Gerdin, David Kerr, Barbara Piper, Erin Potter, Al Ogren, Erik Hansen, Julian Gregory, Gina Pogliano, Melissa Rhines, Meredith McKee, Donnie Mushet, Donnie Popish, and Mark Vogele; David Perry, Jeanne Mackowski, Steve Metcalf, and Rachel Bower, who skillfully turned the reach and power of their marketing work to the issue of our time, with award-winning results; Jeff Hanle, David Clark, Steve Sewell, Peter King, Rob Baxter, Ron Chauner, Doug Mackenzie, Mac Smith, Don Schuster, Hans Hohl, Paul Major, Eric Calderon (who first schooled me in the real world and has accepted my discussions of the challenges at the Nell with good humor and responded with his own green efforts), John Speers, Dennis Steffa, Chris Loan, Gerald Helms, Mark Fitzgerald, Peter Olsen, J. T. Welden, Jim Ward, Peter Hoffman, Gregor Keran (who has told me he "has my back," and I'm grateful), and Paul Cherrett. Joe Nichols helped me understand exactly what was going on over at the Nell in the early days. Over the years, Gardiner Morse at *Harvard Business Review*, Reid Lifeset at the *Journal of Industrial Ecology*, and Hal Clifford and Hannah Fries at *Orion* magazine have helped me think more clearly and get my ideas out to a broader audience. I thank them for permission to use previously published works that appear in various forms in this book. Jim Paussa's family chicken dinners over the course of the year I spent writing the book were indispensible.

With Chris Lane, I've wandered post-bombing Kosovo and skied through vicious snowstorms. He hired me at Aspen Skiing Company and now continues to do excellent environmental work at Xanterra. Hardly a day goes by when we don't discuss our work, our lives, or our next adventure. I'd call him a brother in arms, but he's really just a brother.

My friend Mark Thomas, a hospital chaplain; Dr. Klaus Penzel; Professor Stan Wood at the University of San Francisco; and Father Thomas Keating, who was generous enough to share his time and ideas—all helped me understand the theological and spiritual side of climate change, which is deep and broad enough for another book.

My mother, Mary Jo Schendler, is the ultimate reason for my environmentalism, because she took me away from New Jersey and out to North Dakota in the summers. That place still defines beauty for me. She also let me pursue a ragged and sometimes apparently aimless path that included work as a junk dealer in Steamboat Springs and a fish-packer in Alaska, as well as thousands of miles of hitchhiking, without a critical word, even if my peregrinations might have panicked her at times. Her good common sense, some of which I got—and which she inherited from her father, my Grandpa Joe—should be self-evident in these stories. Grandpa Joe instilled in me the unwavering notion that common sense matters and that work is important and can be an end in itself, if you get something done.

My wife Ellen suffered through drafts and always provided insight and guidance, often in ways that helped me avoid getting in terrible trouble, with the book and otherwise. There are few people in the world who could understand my worldview so well, and I count myself lucky every day to have found her. She, and my children, Willa (who calls me a "goofy global warming guy") and Elias ("Bud"), are, more than anything else, what this book is about.

My agent, Katherine Fausset, recognized that this book had value even when others didn't, and I am grateful for that insight as well as for her continued support, advocacy, and professionalism.

Lindsay Jones, my editor at Public Affairs, is a rare gem indeed: a skilled editor who has thoughtfully and markedly improved this book over a mind-numbing series of revisions. It is vastly better for her efforts, and I thank her for that and for her patience. Susan Weinberg at Public Affairs, along with Lindsay and Katherine, "got" this book in a way I could only have hoped for. Laura Stine and Cindy Buck must have suffered greatly through extensive copy edits, and I thank them for their knowledge of abstruse grammar and the improvements they made. Thanks also to Pete Garceau, Lindsay Goodman, Melissa Raymond, and Dan Ozzi.

Last but not least, my father, David Schendler, with whom I shared too few days, began the process of teaching me how to write and explained to me why it matters. He also told me, over and over again, that I would not be happy unless I was helping people. I hope this book is a leaning in that direction.

AUDEN SCHENDLER is Executive Director of Sustainability at Aspen Skiing Company. He worked previously in corporate sustainability at Rocky Mountain Institute. Auden has been a trailer insulator, burger flipper, ambulance medic, Outward Bound instructor, high school math and English teacher, freelance writer, and Forest Service goose nest island builder. An avid outdoorsman, Auden has climbed Denali, North America's highest peak, and kayaked the Grand Canyon in the winter. His writing has been published in *Harvard Business Review*, the *Los Angeles Times*, *Rock and Ice*, and *Salon.com*, among other places. In 2006, Auden was named a global warming innovator by *Time* magazine. He lives in Basalt, Colorado, with his wife, Ellen, and their children, Willa and Elias.

INDEX

AAA five-diamond auditor, 51–52

Accountability, greenwashing fostering, 230–231

Adaptation for climate change, 122–123

Advertising. *See* Marketing and public relations

Africa, impact of climate change on, 28

Agriculture
biofuels production, 30, 127
climate change affecting, 28

Air quality, 127

Aley, Jack, 216

Algae, 94–95

Alley, Richard, 5

Alliance for Climate Protection, 223

Alternative energy. *See* Renewable energy

American Association for the Advancement of Science, 4

Amicus brief, 92–93

Analysis paralysis, 9–10

Antarctica, 5

Anthropogenic warming, 222

Approval process for greenbuilding, 196

Aqueous parts cleaner, 1, 8–9, 110

Architecture 2030, 185

Aristotle, 135

Aspen, Colorado
as inspiration and demonstration laboratory, 72–74
as metaphor for mainstream America, 74–80
Canary Initiative, 80–83
environmental hypocrisy, 83–85
warming trend, 75–76
See also Aspen Skiing Company; Little Nell Hotel

Aspen Institute, 73

Aspen Skiing Company, 1–2
alternative energy sources, 149–150
amicus brief, 92–93
aqueous parts cleaner, 1, 8–9, 110
biodiesel use, 127–133
commissioning, 140

277

ENVIRONMENTAL BENEFITS STATEMENT

Perseus Books Group saved the following resources by printing the pages of this book on chlorine-free paper made with 100% post-consumer waste.

TREES	WATER	ENERGY	SOLID WASTE	GREENHOUSE GASES
67	24,492	47	3,145	5,901
FULLY GROWN	GALLONS	MILLION BTUs	POUNDS	POUNDS

Calculations based on research by Environmental Defense and the Paper Task Force. Manufactured at Friesens Corporation

PublicAffairs is a publishing house founded in 1997. It is a tribute to the standards, values, and flair of three persons who have served as mentors to countless reporters, writers, editors, and book people of all kinds, including me.

I. F. STONE, proprietor of *I. F. Stone's Weekly*, combined a commitment to the First Amendment with entrepreneurial zeal and reporting skill and became one of the great independent journalists in American history. At the age of eighty, Izzy published *The Trial of Socrates*, which was a national bestseller. He wrote the book after he taught himself ancient Greek.

BENJAMIN C. BRADLEE was for nearly thirty years the charismatic editorial leader of *The Washington Post*. It was Ben who gave the *Post* the range and courage to pursue such historic issues as Watergate. He supported his reporters with a tenacity that made them fearless and it is no accident that so many became authors of influential, best-selling books.

ROBERT L. BERNSTEIN, the chief executive of Random House for more than a quarter century, guided one of the nation's premier publishing houses. Bob was personally responsible for many books of political dissent and argument that challenged tyranny around the globe. He is also the founder and longtime chair of Human Rights Watch, one of the most respected human rights organizations in the world.

· · ·

For fifty years, the banner of Public Affairs Press was carried by its owner Morris B. Schnapper, who published Gandhi, Nasser, Toynbee, Truman, and about 1,500 other authors. In 1983, Schnapper was described by *The Washington Post* as "a redoubtable gadfly." His legacy will endure in the books to come.

Peter Osnos, *Founder and Editor-at-Large*